VOLUME TWO
Comfort From

Meditations

For Such a Time as This

GOSPELS

NORTHWESTERN PUBLISHING HOUSE
Milwaukee, Wisconsin

Library of Congress Card 90-64-162
Northwestern Publishing House
1250 N. 113th St., Milwaukee, WI 53226-3284
© 1991 by Northwestern Publishing House
Published 1991
Printed in the United States of America

CONTENTS

Comfort through Prayer

Comfort for Troubled Hearts

Our Good Shepherd

Living in Peace and Joy

What a Friend We Have in Jesus

The Summons to Glory

On the Road from Grace to Glory

Expectant Christians

EDITOR'S PREFACE

For Such a Time as This. The title of this three volume set of devotions comes from a thought that Mordecai brought to Queen Esther's attention during days of trial and tribulation for the Old Testament people of God. "For such a time as this," Mordecai suggested, God had placed Esther in a position of honor and influence so she could bring God's promised help to God's people (Esther 4:14).

For Such a Time as This. Days of trial and tribulation are no strangers to God's people today. Trials and troubles challenge us, spiritual enemies beset us, fiery trials scorch our faith, our own frailty and mortality frightens us, tragic losses mount, guilt plagues our consciences, personal problems put us on the verge of despair, and sometimes even daily life seems difficult and discouraging.

For Such a Time as This. In times such as these Christians of all ages have turned to God in prayer seeking his help, his promised deliverance, his comfort. They have turned to his Word to find what he has to say to them, and for the past thirty-three years *Meditations* has helped to lead Christians to that comfort of God's Word. Comfort in the fact that God knows who we are, where we are, what we are. Comfort in that God knows the story of our lives and has seen to it through Jesus Christ that it has a happy ending. Comfort in that Jesus has promised to guide us through every trouble, even through the valley of the shadow of death, until we safely stand with him at God's right hand.

For Such a Time as This. Now 300 of those messages of comfort have been selected for inclusion in these three volumes. Each volume contains 100 devotions based on texts chosen from the Gospels, the Epistles, and the Old Testament. Pastor Henry Paustian of Watertown, Wisconsin read through some 12,045 devotions and selected the best of these comfort meditations. Minor changes have been made in some of the original devotions to bring them into line with current procedures. All Scripture quotations and citations are from the NIV; capitalization and punctuation principles reflect current style; titles now are solely the themes of individual devotions instead of a weekly series.

For Such a time as This. Note that on the cover the letters "h-i-s" in the word **this** are printed in another color. That was done to remind all of us that no matter in what situation we may find ourselves, this is still **his,** God's time, that our lives and the events in our lives happen not by chance but under the providential direction of our Father in heaven. As the cover illustration further indicates, we are always safe in his hands.

May the reader find God's comfort in these devotions.

Lyle Albrecht

Who of you by worrying can add a single hour to his life? . . . Therefore do not worry about tomorrow, for tomorrow will worry about itself. Each day has enough trouble of its own. (Matthew 6:27,34)

A LESSON FOR THE WORRIER

You can't change the past, but you can ruin a perfectly good present by worrying about tomorrow. And how many of us haven't let worry ruin a perfectly good day?

Worry brings about results. It brings about ulcers, nervousness, headaches, temper flare-ups and sleepless nights, to name a few. It makes us miserable and unhappy. It creates problems rather than solves them.

Christ teaches us that no one has ever added years to his life by worrying about it. And no one ever will. How foolish, then, to worry! How useless to be anxious!

But how we forget! In our sinfulness we find all kinds of things to worry about. Worry is a sin, and it reveals a lack of trust in God and his providence. A worrying Christian on the one hand acknowledges God's almighty power, but on the other is saying, "I am not so sure you have everything under control, Lord."

We must never forget that God is constant. He doesn't vary. He isn't fickle. He doesn't forget about us, or shortchange us on his blessings. He takes complete care of our lives, every detail and every moment. Worry won't remove sickness, put food on the table, pay bills or solve problems. But God will. He graciously invites us to come to him in prayer and give him all our cares, worries, anxieties, troubles.

Give them to God. Let him take care of them. There is no need to lose sleep at night. There is no need to get ulcers, or lead a miserable existence of fretting and anxiety. God is in control!

Our lives can get pretty hectic and complex, and we may feel we are at the end of our rope. How wonderful to be able to pour out our hearts to God with complete trust in him to take charge and do what's best! Worrying is a sin. Let us give our concerns to God, in prayer.

What a Friend we have in Jesus,
All our sins and griefs to bear!
What a privilege to carry
Everything to God in prayer!
Oh, what peace we often forfeit,
Oh, what needless pain we bear,
All because we do not carry
Everything to God in prayer! Amen.

Now when he saw the crowds, he went up on a mountainside and sat down. His disciples came to him, and he began to teach them, saying: "Blessed are the poor in spirit, for theirs is the kingdom of heaven." (Matthew 5:1-3)

BLESSED ARE THE POOR IN SPIRIT!

When you think of God, do you think of him first as a God who wants to take something from you? Do you think of him first as a God who makes demands?

Jesus teaches us to think of God first as a God who gives, a God who is eager to give us his richest blessings. Jesus came to the people of Galilee, and he comes to us with promises of wonderful blessings. May we gladly receive the blessings our Savior brings!

In his first "beatitude," or word of blessing, Jesus promises God's blessing for all who are poor in spirit.

We can understand what it means to be poor in spirit by thinking about what it means to be poor in body, or physically poor. Many poor people do not have enough food. Many do not have sufficient clothing. Many don't even have a house to live in. They are in need, and they depend on others to give them food, clothing and shelter.

Likewise, people who are poor in spirit are people who are in need. Our souls need to be fed by the Word of God, because man "does not live on bread alone, but on every word that comes from the mouth of God." We are sinners who need to be clothed by God, because "all our righteous acts are like filthy rags." And God in love does clothe us, in the gleaming garments of Christ's righteousness. We need to be sheltered by God because on this earth we have no permanent home. But Jesus gives us a heavenly and eternal home.

Let us be people who are poor in spirit and admit our spiritual needs. Let us turn to Jesus our Savior, who promises to bless us in every spiritual need. He promises to feed us with his Word! He will forgive our sins day by day! He will shelter us in his everlasting arms! Let us also be poor in spirit, because then we will be eternally rich. "Blessed are the poor in spirit," says our Lord, "for theirs is the kingdom of heaven!"

Lord Jesus, thank you for coming to us with promises of wonderful blessings. Help us to know that we are poor and needy in spirit, and help us to turn to you as the only One who can meet our needs. Give us joy in the certainty that ours is the kingdom of heaven. Amen.

Blessed are those who mourn, for they will be comforted. (Matthew 5:4)

BLESSED ARE THOSE WHO MOURN!

I t is sad to see people in mourning who will not be comforted. A woman whose child has died wails in utter and unconsolable grief. A man whose body is wasted by dread disease bemoans the loss of health, job and happiness; he curses God and refuses to be comforted. It is sad to see people thus, because Jesus offers the great blessing of divine comfort for all who mourn.

As children of God we mourn because of our sins. We know the grief they cause our heavenly Father. We know the pain and sorrow they caused our Savior as he suffered and died on the cross. We know the grief they cause our loved ones and ourselves. We mourn because we do not have the strength or ability to overcome our sins, to put them behind us once and for all.

Yes, we mourn because of our sins—but Jesus comforts us in our mourning. He assures us that he loves us in spite of our sins. In fact, he came to this earth for the very purpose of saving just such sinners as we are. He tells us that he has forgiven us—he has washed our sins away in his own blood. He gives us the Holy Spirit, who strengthens us and enables us to bring forth fruits of repentance, and who enables us to live a new and holier life today. Yes, we mourn because of our sins —but in Jesus our Savior we have the forgiveness of sins and eternal salvation!

As children of God we also mourn because of the trials and troubles of life. We are not exempt from these sorrows just because we are Christians. We are not strangers to sickness, death, tragic accidents or personal failure. Jesus said, "In this world you will have trouble," and times of trouble bring grief and mourning. But our eyes need not be blinded by the tears of our mourning. Let us look through the tears and see Jesus at our side! Let us look beyond the sorrows of here and now to the joys of eternity! One day soon our Savior will deliver us from this world of sin. He will wipe all tears from our eyes, and we will be comforted! Surely we mourn because of our sins, and surely we mourn because of the troubles of life, but in all our mourning the Savior's promise holds true: "Blessed are those who mourn, for they will be comforted!"

Lord Jesus, thank you for the comforting message of the gospel. Comfort us in all our griefs, and help us bring the comfort of your love to others. Amen.

3

"Who of you by worrying can add a single cubit to his height?"
(Matthew 6:27)

NO PROFIT IN WORRY

A mother worries about her son who is out with his friends on a Friday night. She knows that he is a good, responsible boy, but she worries nevertheless. So many things could happen to him.

Her husband worries about his job. Will the problems at the shop continue to increase until he is forced to look for other work? Where will he find something that pays enough to meet all the family expenses .

The son, a junior in high school, worries about his grades. Suppose he doesn't pass the last chemistry test! Will he fail the course? If he fails, will he be able to go on to college?

His older sister is off at the university now and finds the classes quite easy. But she worries about not finding someone suitable to marry. She is already 20 years old and has no steady boy friend.

This family is far more typical than it ought to be. They represent many sleepless hours, countless helpings of good food pushed back on the table, and hours upon hours of irritableness.

But what are father, mother, son and daughter accomplishing by their worry? About as much as they would accomplish if each of them by their powers of concentration were trying to grow an inch. Worry does not solve problems. It only adds to our woes.

Enough of such foolishness. Let us commit our way to the Lord and trust in him. He will bring matters to a successful conclusion for us. He will watch over Junior while he is out with his friends and will guide him into the right career, whether it be through a college education or not. He will find Sis a good husband, if in his wisdom he chooses to join her to a man in holy matrimony. Unless the Lord knows that it is best to lay a heavy cross on the whole family, father will continue to be able to support his wife, his children and himself.

In every case, whether things work out exactly as we hope or some other way, our heavenly Father is sending us those things only which he knows to be in our best interest. He knows our needs, and he knows best how to meet them so that we may remain his children.

Let us step back and give our dear Father room to work. Our brains were made for solving the problems that are within our reach, not those beyond our control. Our hearts were made for faith and love, not for anxiety. Let the Lord add the cubits to our stature. He knows how tall we should be.

Dear Lord, deliver us from sinful, painful worry. Amen.

Therefore I tell you, do not worry about your life, what you will eat or drink, or about your body, what you will wear. Is not life more important than food, and the body more important than clothes? Look at the birds of the air; they do not sow or reap or store away in barns, and yet your heavenly Father feeds them. Are you not much more valuable than they? (Matthew 6:25,26)

A LESSON FROM LITTLE BIRDS

If you ever need some cheering up, and you want to hear someone with an optimistic viewpoint, just watch and listen to some birds. Birds by their very nature are carefree, lightspirited, happy creatures. Martin Luther pictured little birds as "live saints" who sing praises to God without the least worry and are fed by him day by day.

God expects us to work for a living, using wisely his gifts for our good. Birds aren't expected to work. For them there is no seedtime or harvest. They have no barns or granaries in which they store food. But their tables are always set. Sometimes they have the choicest food, sometimes just enough to sustain life. But they eat, because God takes care of them!

How foolish we would be not to learn from them! We have the same almighty God, only our relationship is a deeper one, because he is our heavenly Father and we are his dear children. He loves us and will give us everything we need. After all, he gave us our body. How could he fail to take care of its nourishment?

But as sinful creatures we many times put our noses to the grindstone and forget to look up to our Provider. We may worry about what we will eat, how long we will keep our job, whether or not we can afford our house payment. Such anxiety over our physical necessities shows a lack of trust in the Giver of all things. Worrying indicates that we are trying to make it alone, forgetting that all things come from God. In our sinfulness, Christ comes to us with the example of the little birds, and tells us to cast our cares upon him and he will care for us. May we trust in him without hesitation, resting on his providence.

What is the world to me!
My Jesus is my Treasure,
My Life, my Health, my Wealth,
My Friend, my Love, my Pleasure,
My Joy, my Crown, my All,
My Bliss eternally.
Once more, then, I declare:
What is the world to me! Amen.

"Therefore I tell you, do not worry about your life, what you will eat or drink; or about your body, what you will wear. Is not life more important than food, and the body more important than clothes? Look at the birds of the air; they do not sow or reap or store away in barns, and yet your heavenly Father feeds them. Are you not much more valuable than they?" (Matthew 6:25,26)

GOD PROVIDES

Many times we feel we don't have everything we need. We need a new car and the money just isn't there. That living-room chair is ready to fall apart. The room addition we had planned —well, there's no need of even thinking of it now. And we could go on. We never have enough.

But is this true? Are we really lacking the things we need? What is meant by "need"? It varies from one person to another. If we examine the situation, we will probably find that the things we don't have are things we really don't need. The old car really could be repaired. We don't absolutely need the room addition. And we do have other chairs in the living room. The things we really need, the basic necessities of life we still have. God has never failed to give us these.

God has actually given us more than the basic things in life. We have television sets, boats and "convenience foods." Many of our families have two cars. We take pleasant vacations. If we are honest, we must admit that God has given us many luxuries.

Our text, however, is not mainly concerned with luxuries. It speaks of basic necessities. Jesus says, "Don't be concerned about even the basic things. The Father will give them to you." He assures us of this promise when he says, "Is not life more important than food, and the body more important than clothes?" In other words, if God has given us the greater gift, life, won't he also give us the lesser gift, our food? If he has given us the greater gift, our body, won't he also give us the lesser gift, clothing for our body? He also refers to birds. Martin Luther pictures birds as "live saints who sing their praise to God without the least worry and are fed by him day after day." They cannot do what we can do, namely, sow seed, harvest the fruit and store it for the future. Yet God takes care of them. Certainly, we are much higher in his eyes than the birds. He'll care for us.

Dear heavenly Father, you care for us so much that you provide us with everything we need. Help us to remember that, and not be too much concerned about our physical welfare. Amen.

And why do you worry about clothes? See how the lilies of the field grow. They do not labor or spin. Yet I tell you that not even Solomon in all his splendor was dressed like one of these. If that is how God clothes the grass of the field, which is here today and tomorrow is thrown into the fire, will he not much more clothe you, O you of little faith? So do not worry, saying "What shall we eat?" or "What shall we drink?" or "What shall we wear?" For the pagans run after all these things, and your heavenly Father knows that you need them. (Matthew 6:28-32)

A LESSON FROM THE LILIES

What a beautiful lesson our Savior teaches us! What a simple lesson from the flowers of the field! Christ directs us to one of the flowers commonly seen in Palestine—a pretty lily that thrived without cultivation.

Its beauty was such that even Solomon, in the splendor of his attire, could not be compared with it.

While the natives of Palestine burned these little flowers for fuel and held them in low esteem, God esteemed them enough to clothe them in splendid colors, more gorgeous than the apparel of Israel's richest king. Even these little flowers were in his almighty care.

Are we also not cared for? Yet, are we not often anxious about the clothing we need, and the other necessities of life? We worry about being without, even though God has seen fit to put us into a land of plenty, in the midst of abundance. Such worrying is a sure indicator that our faith needs a boost.

Christ teaches us to find comfort in the fact that our heavenly Father knows what we need. He takes care of everything. The ungodly worship the god of materialism. The child of God is to know better, and not be identified with such a spirit.

There is nothing wrong with seeking after food, clothing and a place to live. God wants us to work faithfully and provide for ourselves and others. But Christ cautions us not to give our hearts to these things and make them our dearest treasures in life. Much more important is raiment for our soul, the robe of Christ's righteousness, with which God covers our rags of sin. Seek after this clothing for your soul, revealed in the gospel of God's love in Jesus, and you have the clothing that lasts for eternity.

I am trusting Thee to guide me;
Thou alone shalt lead,
Ev'ry day and hour supplying
All my need. Amen.

Are not two sparrows sold for a penny? Yet not one of them will fall to the ground apart from the will of your Father. And even the very hairs of your head are all numbered. So don't be afraid; you are worth more than many sparrows. (Matthew 10:29-31)

DARE TO TRUST!

The daring discipleship to which Jesus calls each Christian is full of challenges. Meeting them often means suffering. The faithful disciple cannot help but be opposed by the forces of Satan in many forms.

As we accept the challenges of our Christian faith, we need God's care. If physical persecution is absent, we still have to deal with being called unloving, antagonistic, divisive and prejudiced by the unbelieving world. All this and more afflicts the daring disciple.

We have to add to that inner challenges. No Christian is completely free from feelings of doubt. Sin rears its ugly head and attempts to kill each disciple's hope. Even our failures to live up to Christ's challenges to daring discipleship gnaw at our hearts.

In this desperate situation we have an all-powerful Lord who cares. We can see how he provides for and watches over the creatures of this world. Not even sparrows, which seem so valueless at times, are outside of his concern. "Not one of them will fall to the ground apart from the will of your Father."

From that we can be sure that God also cares for our physical well-being. All the hairs of our heads are numbered. Not one of them is lost apart from our heavenly Father's will either.

Just think, if God cares so much about our bodies, how much more must he care about our eternal souls! In this truth, Jesus challenges, actually invites, us to trust in God for everything.

He sits at the Father's right hand to watch over our every physical and spiritual need. He knows firsthand the challenges we face. He was tempted. He was afflicted. He was despised.

And Jesus will provide. He cared enough to die for us on the cross. He loved us enough to shed his blood to pay for our sins.

He gives strength for every moment of weakness. He sends joy for every sorrow. He grants peace for every trouble.

This challenge to be daring disciples is really no challenge at all. God graciously supplies the strength, the faith to accept his gracious promises. Let us simply put our trust in him.

I am trusting Thee, Lord Jesus;
Never let me fall.
I am trusting Thee forever
And for all. Amen.

"And do not set your heart on what you will eat or drink; do not worry about it. For the pagan world runs after all such things, and your Father knows that you need them. But seek his kingdom, and these things will be given to you as well. "(Luke 12:29-31)

THE ONLY VALID PRIORITY

The world is full of such who do not believe. But that's not all. Christians also live in this world. And like the unbelievers, Christians have a great need for "things." Things like a job to provide income, food for nourishment, clothing for warmth, homes for shelter and families for happiness. And as long as Christians are in this world, these needs will daily continue to confront them.

The difference is that the unbeliever thinks that these things are all that count in life. The Christian, on the other hand, knows that he needs something else even more. As important as it is to provide an education for our children, to establish a good and enjoyable family life and to obtain all the luxuries that somehow have become necessities, the Christian has an even deeper yearning for that which Jesus Christ alone can give. That is the assurance of God's love, the joy of forgiveness and the hope of everlasting salvation. Only Jesus can offer this, because Jesus is the only Savior whom God sent to make it all possible. It happened on the cross.

Ever since the day he came, Jesus has tried to impress on his followers that if we put him first on our list of needs, everything else will be taken care of by God. And we will never have to worry for one minute about our bodily needs. That's an overwhelming promise. But it's reliable, because it comes from Jesus—from Jesus who was sent by the Father in heaven and came to take our place.

Come next Christmas, many of us will be looking for a bonus from our boss. A bonus is "something extra." And that's what Jesus offers us here: a bonus, something extra. "Seek ye the kingdom of God and all these things shall be added unto you." It is as though Jesus said, "Hold on to me and cling to me as your Savior. Trust me when I tell you that my blood covers all your sins. Make heaven the first goal of your life. Give priority to the needs of your soul, for they are your greatest needs. And I promise—on God's honor—that you will always have everything that you will ever need for your body." What a promise! What a blessed freedom from worry if we only believe it!

Dear Savior, help me keep you first in my life, to make the concerns of your kingdom my priority. Amen.

Then Jesus said to his disciples: "Therefore I tell you, do not worry about your life, what you will eat; or about your body, what you will wear. Life is more than food, and the body more than clothes. . . . And do not set your heart on what you will eat or drink; do not worry about it. For the pagan world runs after all such things, and your Father knows that you need them. But seek his kingdom, and these things will be given to you as well." (Luke 12:22,23,29-31)

CAST CARE ASIDE!

There are feelings and attitudes which do not conflict with our Christianity. One attitude, however, is under all circumstances completely at odds with our creed and conviction. It is worry. That is why our Lord exhorts us, "Do not worry about your life." That is why the Lord's Apostle Paul encourages us, "Do not be anxious about anything" (Philippians 4:6).

This world of sin is a vast breeding ground for all sorts of cares. People worry about their daily bread and daily job, about their debts or investments, about sickness and the health of their bodies, about sin and the state of their souls. They worry about their parents or children, about husband or wife, about their country and community, about their church and congregation. Such cares seek to invade and to infest every home and heart. All of them are included in the warning word, "Do not worry about it!"

When all is said and done, all these cares come from a single source and acquire weight through the same burden. This common source and burden is sin. Christ came to take away our sin. Our faith in him makes us free from care and worry. He is our burden-bearer. God our Father took the whole ugly burden of our guilt and cast it upon his Son, our Savior. For the sake of that Son and Savior our Father invites us to cast the whole heavy burden of our care upon him.

Between his first and second comings, Christ's believers need never anxiously ask, "What shall we eat or drink or wear?" They can trust that the faithful Lord, who sent them the Savior, will also with that Savior freely give them all things. They can cast care away. They can cast it, with the strong arm of faith and with hands folded for prayer, on the eternal, almighty, omniscient, merciful, loving Lord who cares for them.

"So be it," then I say
With all my heart each day,
We, too, dear Lord, adore thee,
We sing for joy before thee.
Guide us while here we wander
Until we praise thee yonder. Amen.

"So he got up and went to his father. But while he was still a long way off, his father saw him and was filled with compassion for him; he ran to his son, threw his arms around him and kissed him. The son said to him, 'Father, I have sinned against heaven and against you. I am no longer worthy to be called your son.' But the father said to his servants, 'Quick! Bring the best robe and put it on him. Put a ring on his finger and sandals on his feet. Bring the fattened calf and kill it. Let's have a feast and celebrate. For this son of mine was dead and is alive again; he was lost and is found.' So they began to celebrate." (Luke 15:20-24)

THIS IS HOW GOD IS

Everyone has favorite people. My favorite people are a supermarket stocker, a mailman, a Sunday school teacher and a man and woman who sit across the aisle from each other on Sunday mornings. Each has a smile on his face and a twinkle in his eye. A person feels good because they are glad to see you, to talk to you, to be with you. The son in our Scripture reading discovered that he had a father like that.

Earlier in Jesus' parable, the boy had decided he could manage his life without the help of Father, Mother or God. He had left home with his share of his father's wealth and made a disaster of his life. When all was gone, he came to his senses and decided to return home. He would confess all and plead, even beg, for a chance to be a menial servant in the house. But he didn't know his father well. The father ran out to meet him, forgave him everything and celebrated his return with a joyous feast.

Jesus told this parable so that we would know that the smile on the father's face, his open arms and his joy are pictures of God as he receives a sinner who repents.

A person might get the idea from watching certain Christians that we are supposed to be sad, longfaced people. It is good to be serious about worship, but Jesus wants us to know that God meets us like that father in the parable. God has open arms for us when we admit our sins and come to him for help. God provides us with a beautiful robe, the robe of Jesus' righteousness. He invites us to a splendid feast, the feast of his Word and his Sacrament. What love!

When we, on our part, know that God loves us like this, we, too, will reflect his love in a big smile on our face as we meet, work and play with people. Happy Christians ought to be everybody's favorite people because through Christians other people learn that God forgives and loves them, too.

Heavenly Father, let us never lose sight of your open arms. Draw us back to you if we stray. Let the inner joy we feel light our faces and draw others to the warmth of your love. Amen.

"For God so loved the world that he gave his one and only Son, that whoever believes in him shall not perish but have eternal life." (John 3:16)

REJOICE IN THE GOSPEL OF GOD'S LOVE

There is beauty in simplicity. Some of the most beautiful and precious truths of our Christian faith are expressed in language so simple that even a child can understand them. The familiar and beloved verse before us today is a classic example.

It tells us that God, the holy and righteous Lord of all, loved the world—notice, "loved" not "liked," for how could God like a sinful, foul, stinking world? But he could and did love it, love all the poor, miserable sinners in it, love it so much that he gave his one and only Son. He gave him to be born, to live, to suffer and die and rise again for the world's redemption. He gave him to pay in full for all the sins of all the sinners, so that whoever believes in him—and here everyone of us is invited to write in his or her own name—shall not perish but have eternal life. That's the simple, beautiful, great good news that Jesus brought to Nicodemus and that he brings to us.

To be sure, this good news of the gospel is foolishness to natural man. To human reason it seems all wrong that God should sacrifice his Son to save sinners of every kind, that publicans and harlots who repent and believe in him shall not perish, while respectable people who try to do what is right are condemned if they do not believe. But this is the offense of the gospel, the fact that salvation is entirely by God's grace and not by man's goodness.

But in this offense of the gospel lies also its greatest glory, for the gospel doesn't demand, it gives. It doesn't require that we meet God halfway, but assures us that he went all the way for us. It offers eternal life to infants who cannot yet do any good works and to old sinners who have broken God's law again and again. It takes hold of publicans like Matthew and harlots like Rahab, and by the power of the Holy Spirit operating through it makes them repentant and believing saints. It gives the thief on the cross the sure hope of heaven, and it gives you and me, as vile as he, that same hope and fills us with all joy and peace in believing.

That's the gospel, the simple but surpassingly beautiful good news that is at the very heart of Christianity. May we never grow tired of hearing it but rejoice in it daily and share it eagerly.

Lord, you have revealed your saving grace in beautiful simplicity. Help us to rejoice in it with a simple, childlike faith. Amen.

"For God so loved. . . . Just as Moses lifted up the snake in the desert, so the Son of Man must be lifted up." (John 3:16,14)

GOD WROTE THE BOOK ON LOVE

How do you show love for God? We can't see him. We know he's there, but we don't have that face-to-face relationship with him that would allow us to exhibit our love for him in the ways we can for family or friends.

It helps first to identify just what kind of love we're talking about. If we want to know what love is and how to show it, we should ask God, because "God is love," the Bible says. He is the author of love. He wrote the book on love.

And not being content with merely lecturing the world on the subject of love, he put his love into action. He sent us love in the form of his own Son, Jesus Christ. Jesus loves us with more than just a friendship kind of love, although he certainly is our friend. To help us understand his love for us, Scripture calls him the bridegroom and the church his bride.

Jesus' love is more than a feeling or emotion. His is the "doing" kind of love. Jesus loved us and died for us before we ever learned the first lesson on love. We became Christians, not because we loved God, but because God first loved us. His love prompted him to take steps toward our salvation before we even knew we needed saving.

Already in Moses' day God revealed his plans for our salvation in some striking ways. When, for example, the Israelites were dying in the desert after being bitten by poisonous snakes, Moses, at God's bidding, lifted up a bronze serpent for them to look at and be cured. Their looking didn't save them. It was the power of God's promise associated with their looking.

This Old Testament episode was a preview of how God in love would one day let his Son be lifted up on a cross and how that Son's death would be the remedy for all sin. We must look to Calvary for eternal life. Just as the Israelite was saved with a look, so the sinner is saved by looking to Jesus.

We call that the great exchange, when God substituted his Son's life for us worthless sinners. Isaiah 53 tells the whole story: "Surely he took up our infirmities and carried our sorrows . . . the Lord has laid on him the iniquity of us all." God had one perfect Son. He was willing to give that one and only Son, that he might one day have a whole kingdom of sons and daughters.

Through faith in Christ you are one of God's children, and God finds many ways to show his love for you. You are dear to him. When you are feeling worthless and blue, remember that God loved you so much that he sacrificed his only begotten Son to redeem you.

Father, how can you love us so much? Teach us your kind of love, that we may be more like you. Amen.

"For God so loved the world that he gave his one and only Son, that whoever believes in him shall not perish but have eternal life." (John 3:16)

GOD LOVES THE WORLD—GREAT NEWS!

I f you circle the first letter of the 2d word, the 11th, the 14th, the 22d, the 25th and the 26th words in the Bible verse above, they spell gospel. John 3:16 is often called "the gospel in a nutshell" since it tells you the good—no, make that the greatest—news you could ever hope to hear: GOD LOVES THE WORLD!

Since you are part of the world, God loves you! In spite of your sins, he does not disqualify you from his kingdom. Instead he gave his Son to be your Savior. Isn't that good news? God doesn't want anyone to suffer eternal punishment in hell. He wants you to spend your forever life with him and his Son in heaven.

Once you have read John 3:16, you need never again doubt God's feelings toward you. Whoever believes will not perish but will live forever.

The word whoever appears in God's Book 179 times. Whenever the term applies to salvation, it means "anyone without exception."

Contrary to God's wishes, there will be some, come judgment day, who will be condemned, but it will be their will, not God's. If God had his way, everyone would respond to the good news, repent and be saved.

If you still have your doubts, read John 3:16 again. This time insert your own name where it says "the world" and "whoever." "For God so loved . . . that he gave his one and only Son that . . . believes in him [and] shall not perish but have eternal life." Thanks to Jesus and his cross your name is also written in "the Lamb's book of life." That's good news!

The "good news" for others is that there still is room. God once lifted up his Son, whose death is God's remedy for sin. It is now our mission to "lift up" the Messiah that the world might see and believe. God loves the cosmos.

This coming week tell that good news to someone you meet who may not yet know his or her Savior. Pray that God will give you opportunities to tell and supply the words you need to share the good news. Jesus once said, "I have other sheep that are not of this sheep pen. I must bring them also." God so loved them too; they just don't know about it yet.

Dear God, when doubts about my salvation appear in my mind and heart, send me back to your good news. Send me back to John 3:16, which says it all, for me and for everyone. Amen.

"For God so loved the world that he gave. . . ." (John 3:16)

THE WORLD'S GREATEST ACT OF LOVE

A runner in a marathon race crosses the line and finishes fourth. "He gave it his all," his coach says. A little girl's eyes widen as she sees her dad open his wallet and take out all the cash—four $20s —and drop it into the offering plate in church. "He gave all his money," she thinks to herself. But in these examples it isn't really "all." It may be a lot, but for the runner there's always a little more strength and energy to draw upon; otherwise he would drop over dead. The dad isn't really broke or bankrupt; there's money in savings he could use and there's another paycheck coming soon.

But when God gave, he did "give his all." He gave with no reservations; there were no back-up Sons to send later. He has only one Son, and yet he willingly gave him up to be the world's Savior from sin. God gave the most lavish gift the world has ever seen. He gave this gift to you and me. Because his gift was perfect for you, solving all your basic spiritual needs—forgiveness of sins, life, salvation, freedom from guilt and then some—you surely want to give God a gift in return. You can do that! St. Paul tells you to live your whole life as a gift to God by dedicating everything you do to his glory. But remember! You're not doing this to earn your way into God's good graces. You are merely saying, "Thank you, God. You really did give your all so that I could be yours."

Everything about God's gift was unique. No one else compares with God's Son. Nothing else compares with his act of salvation. Never before and never since Jesus has a baby been born of a virgin. Ever since Adam no man except Jesus lived an absolutely sin-free life. No one else has been able to do the miracles he did. If other individuals died for the sake of another, their sacrifice, no matter how noble, did nothing about sin. Not one person who has died has ever come back from death on his own.

And, finally, Jesus' resurrection was the absolute proof that in him and in what he did God accomplished for us what we could never hope to do on our own—overcome sin and death and make us fit for heaven.

God "gave his all" because he loves you. When a woman told her pastor that she did not think she was saved because she did not love God enough, the pastor simply replied, "That doesn't matter. He loves you." Engrave these words in your memory. Hang them on the wall on your heart. God loves you. The cross is all the proof you need.

Dear Father, when I worry about being saved, remove all anxiety and care from my heart. Help me remember each day that in Jesus you love me. That will never change and nothing else really matters. Motivate me to return your love in all I think, say and do. Amen.

The soldiers led Jesus away into the palace (that is, the Praetorium) and called together the whole company of soldiers. They put a purple robe on him. (Mark 15:16,17)

HIS ROBE

"The royal purple" people called it in days gone by. In olden days kings and queens wore robes of purple, for only they could afford the costly dye required in making such robes. The purple robe then became a symbol of the magnificent palaces, gilded chariots and rich splendor which surrounded royalty.

That Good Friday in Pilate's palace another king wore the royal purple. But what a king he was and what a robe he wore! Some soldier had found it in some corner of the barracks and draped it over Jesus' naked shoulders. And if the color was somewhat faded, that didn't matter. It would soon be darkened again by the blood from his torn back. A king he was supposed to be, so with coarse taunts the soldiers outfitted him like one, in a purple robe stained by his own blood.

They placed the robe on his back in mockery that day, but a moment's worth of deeper reflection will show how fitting it was. If anyone could wear "the royal purple," Jesus could. Let earthly kings have their halls of marble and homes of splendor, Jesus had the Father's house above. Let earthly kings fill their closets with fashion's latest, he had the heavenly brightness which dazzled his disciples on the Mount of Transfiguration. Let earthly kings struggle to win and hold their paltry kingdoms, he made and rules over all.

And yet he must wear a cheap, cast-off cloak. This King of kings has chosen to leave behind heaven's splendor for a life on earth as a humble servant. He who owns all has to borrow a place to lay his head, a boat to cross a lake, a cape to cloak his body, a tomb to hold his corpse. Willingly he chooses to endure poverty and pain, self-denial and death. Never has the world seen royalty like this!

That bloodstained robe reminds us of his royalty. It reminds us also of something else. How he must love us! All this he endured to pay for our sins, rescue us from hell, equip us for heaven. All this he endured to weave another robe, the robe of his righteousness which he drapes over our shoulders. Because of that robe we can stand before our God in heaven and even rule with him, our King, forever.

"King," they said in mockery that day. "King, indeed!" we respond as he puts the robe of righteousness on us, "King of kings and Lord of lords!"

Jesus, thy blood and righteousness
My beauty are, my glorious dress;
Midst flaming worlds, in these arrayed,
With joy shall I lift up my head. Amen.

They . . . twisted together a crown of thorns and set it on him. (Mark 15:17)

HIS CROWN

Earthly kings wear crowns, some of them simple circles of gold, others elaborate rings studded with gems. From Egypt's ancient dynasties to Europe's modern monarchs, the sovereign wears a crown.

King Jesus must also have a crown, so the mocking soldiers thought. A prickly branch was found, twined together, and placed on his royal head. But it lacked the sparkle of precious stones. No problem; that could easily be supplied. A few blows on that circle of thorns brought drops of his blood to glisten like rubies.

They placed that crown of thorns on his brow in mockery that day, but a moment's worth of deeper reflection will show how fitting it was. Let others wear golden crowns with cold and lifeless gems, Jesus wears a crown adorned with his own blood, blood more precious than all earth's treasures, blood able to win that which nothing else could buy. That crown, touched with his blood, speaks of victory, victory over sin, death and the devil.

Only victors wear crowns, and Jesus hardly looked like a victor that day. Yet Easter Sunday brought news of victory complete. And now in heaven the Victor rules. In heaven the angels who have ever been there and the saints who have gone before us join in the chorus, "Worthy is the Lamb, who was slain, to receive power and wealth and wisdom and strength and honor and glory and praise!"

Shall we not join them? Can we be silent while angels sing the great Redeemer's praise? Is it not rather, "Oh, that with yonder sacred throng we at his feet may fall. We'll join the everlasting song and crown him Lord of all"? Why wait for heaven to crown our eternal King? The time to start is now! Let's give him the throne room in our hearts. Let's daily retake that oath of allegiance to him that we first spoke on our confirmation day. Let's sing with the heroes of old to that King of Creation, "Truly I'd love thee, truly I'd serve thee, Light of my soul, my Joy, my Crown."

May that Savior, whose sacred head was scornfully surrounded with thorns as his only crown, forgive our frequent lack of loyalty and fainthearted service to him. May he move us to surrender our hearts and lives in willing homage to him.

"King," they said in mockery that day. "King, indeed!" we respond as he offers us the crown of glory, "King of kings and Lord of lords!"

Dear Jesus, give us hearts of faith to hold you and lives of love to serve you all our days. Amen.

And they began to call out to him, "Hail, king of the Jews!" Again and again they struck him on the head with a staff and spit on him. Falling on their knees, they paid homage to him. (Mark 15:18,19)

HIS HOMAGE

The crowds cheered and the flags waved as we stood on the main avenue in Mexico City on November 20, the anniversary of their revolution, and watched as the president of Mexico went by. Rulers are used to receiving homage from their people.

King Jesus also must have homage, so the cruel soldiers thought. "Hail, king of the Jews!" they mocked, bowing low before him. Then they spit on him. Disgusting, dirty spittle for his face, such was the homage considered worthy for this king. Others amused themselves snatching the reed from his hand and rapping him over the head with it. Such was the respect they had for this king.

They bowed before him in mockery that day, but how fitting homage is for this king. Before them stood one who was more than just Jesus, the Son of Mary. He was Jesus, the sinless, almighty Son of God, co-ruler of heaven and earth. One word from his lips and angels could have flocked to his defense. One sentence and rough soldiers would have sprawled on the pavement. One glance and Pilate would have been rendered powerless.

They were manhandling the King of kings. Finally they would even put him on the cross, not because he couldn't stop them, but because he didn't want to. His love wouldn't let him stop them. In love he was "laying down his life for the sheep," just as he said he would. Here's the true glory of our King! Willingly he lays down his life for the sins of the world that we might inherit an eternal kingdom.

So where are our cheers and flags? Certainly we want to be on our knees before him, sending prayers and praises to him. But that's the easy part. Far more difficult is it to keep on waving those flags and shouting those praises in the daily routine we call life. Let our fellow church members see by the way we worship him each Sunday; let our family members see by the way we lead them daily to this throne; let our fellow workers see by the way we dedicate workday matters to him that we know who our King is, what he has done for us and how worthy he is to receive our homage.

"King," they said in mockery that day. "King indeed!" we respond as we serve him in his kingdom, "King of kings and Lord of lords!"

Dear Jesus, remind us of the kingdom which is ours through your innocent suffering and death, that we may serve you willingly. Amen.

And when they had mocked him, they took off the purple robe and put his own clothes on him. Then they led him out to crucify him. (Mark 15:20)

HIS THRONE

Kings must have their thrones as seats of honor and proof of power. In the royal palace in Madrid, Spain, stands such a throne, overlaid with the richest gold and upholstered with the finest velvet.

King Jesus also had his throne, a most unlikely one at that. It was a seat reserved for the worst criminal, the lowest slave, and God's Son! Today we bronze it and position it on our altars. We gild it and put it on chains. We polish it and place it on our steeples. But in Jesus' day it meant the worst disgrace and the deepest pain.

Who can describe the pain of rough nails tearing through flesh as nerve endings screamed out? Who can lay out in words what it meant to hang on that rough wood and wait for life to ebb slowly, all too slowly, from a pain-wracked body? Still worse, who can plumb the depths of what it meant for Jesus to have hell's punishment wash over him, one crashing wave after the other, as payment for every sin in the world was demanded? Who can detail what it meant for him to drink that cup of suffering to its bitter end on the cross where he was enthroned?

Even more—who can fully describe the love behind it all? Love is never easy to define, the love of parent for child, lover for spouse, friend for another. But love that would bring God down from his glorious throne on high where he was surrounded by angels to be enthroned on a cross and encircled by thieves, where do we find the words? In John 15:13 the King told his disciples, "Greater love has no one than this, that one lay down his life for his friends." Later, one of those disciples, after having stood beneath the King's cross, wrote, "This is how we know what love is: Jesus Christ laid down his life for us." And that love becomes even more indescribable when we realize Christ died not for friends, but for enemies.

Earthly monarchs can have their thrones of gold and velvet. The cross of our King is infinitely more beautiful and far more valuable. For the believer that cross spells God's love and the sinner's salvation in shining letters. For the believer that cross is his Savior's glorious throne.

"King," they said in mockery that day as they lifted him up on the cross. "King indeed!" we respond as we kneel in humble thanks before our Savior on his throne of love, "King of kings and Lord of lords!"

Dear Jesus, draw us to your cross in life and death. Amen.

While they were eating, Jesus took bread, gave thanks and broke it and gave it to his disciples, saying, "Take it; this is my body." Then he took the cup, gave thanks and offered it to them, and they all drank from it. "This is my blood of the covenant, which is poured out for many," he said to them. (Mark 14:22-24)

HIS LEGACY

Kings work mightily to extend the borders of their realms and enlarge their riches. They want more for themselves and more to leave as legacies for their children. But so often earth's riches are ripped from their grasp or squandered by their descendants.

King Jesus also has a legacy for us. And he worked hard to get it. It took him to the cross to give up his life in payment for the world's sins. Forgiveness was the rich treasure he would win and leave for all people.

This forgiveness our King offers in a very special way. As he ate the Passover with his disciples on the night before he went to Calvary, he left his forgiveness in a unique form. Taking the unleavened bread and the cup of wine on the table, he gave them to his disciples and said, "Take it; this is my body. . . . This is my blood of the covenant." Miraculously, but really, he gave them his body and blood along with that bread and wine to assure them of the forgiveness of all their sins.

What a legacy! Jesus knew how often his followers would be weak and wobbly, how often their faith would flicker and fade, how often they would need to be assured of forgiveness. So he gave them the miracle of his Holy Supper. In that Supper along with the bread and the wine he gives us the very body and blood he used to prepare forgiveness. Who can doubt that sins are gone and heaven opened as he receives the very body and blood of his Savior?

What do you do with a legacy? Lock it away in a bank vault or stash it on a closet shelf? Far better when new sins alarm us and old guilt won't let go, far better when faith needs feeding and Christian muscles cry out for strengthening, to stand at his table and to hear him tell us again, "Here, this is my body; I gave it for YOU. Here, this is my blood; I shed it for YOU. YOUR sins are forgiven. YOU depart in peace."

Our King has left us a wondrous legacy. As we use it regularly, we can't help but exclaim, "He's a King indeed! He's King of kings and Lord of lords!"

Dear Jesus, let your Holy Supper refresh us today and often. Amen.

With that, he bowed his head and gave up his spirit. (John 19:30)

HIS DEATH

Television programs are interrupted for special bulletins. Reporters come from afar when one of earth's royalty dies and is buried.

That Good Friday another King died. His soul left its home in his body. His head dropped down; his cheeks turned pale; his eyes lost their luster. Those who watched realized he was dead just like so many kings before and after him.

Yet his death was different. Death is always something solemn. When we stand at a deathbed, we feel God's nearness and realize he's speaking to us. If true with the death of an ordinary mortal, how much more so when the God-man closes his eyes? If we can feel the deep mystery in human dying, how much more so when the everlasting Christ hangs dead on the cross? With the hymnwriter we have to marvel, "O sorrow dread, God's Son is dead."

The King who died was different; so was the way he died. We know why we die. It's because we have to. We may want to live longer, but our strength gives out, our heart stops, and we die. Nothing on earth can add one second to our life. With Jesus it was far different. He was not dying because he was powerless to stop the process. He was dying because he loved us and wanted to die for us. He even set the time of his death, for we are told, "He gave up his spirit." Death did not capture Jesus, but he went forward to meet it. He who once said, "I lay down my life—only to take it up again. No one takes it from me, but I lay it down of my own accord," now proved this fact as he committed his soul into the hands of his heavenly Father.

And we? Yes, we must die. Yes, there is nothing we can do about it. But because of Jesus' death, for us death is no longer the king of terrors and the unbeatable foe. When God's children must give up their souls, they hand them over to no stranger or enemy, but into the loving hands of an eternal Father. He will take us home safely to those mansions prepared by his Son on Calvary's cross.

Our King died that day. No television shows were interrupted and no reporters came. But his death has meant life for thousands like us and ever will.

Must we not say it, "A King indeed! Yes, King of kings and Lord of lords!"

Dear Savior, let your triumphant death be my comfort now and in the hour of my death. Amen.

When he had received the drink, Jesus said, "It is finished." (John 19:30)

HIS VICTORY

I t was early morning, May 7, 1945. Some of us can remember the day. Five years, eight months and seven days after war had been declared with Germany, it was over. Victory was ours!

It was close to 3:00 on a Friday afternoon about A.D. 30. All of us need to remember that day. The war was over, one raging ever since sin had closed Eden's door. And the victory was ours!

Out on Calvary scarcely had the sponge soaked with sour wine moistened our King's lips when he spoke. "It is finished," he said. One word of four syllables in Greek, and yet it was the most important word the world would ever hear. The Greeks wrote this word on tax bills to show that they were paid in full. Now our Savior shouted it from his cross. What did it mean? What was over?

Jesus did not speak in the whisper of dying men which you must lean low to hear. No, he spoke, as the Gospel writer tells us, with "a loud voice" so that all might hear. He shouted, "I have won! My work of salvation is done. I have kept the law perfectly for all people. I have paid for all sins, not one remains. I have suffered the agonies of hell which were reserved for sinners. I have endured the full punishment and righteous anger of my Father over sin. I have shed my precious blood to redeem all mankind. And now it, my work of salvation, is completely finished." Our precious Savior from his position on the cross could turn his gaze from the first sinner to the last and see no one for whom he had not paid.

Talk about victory! Does our conscience tell us, "You are a great sinner and deserve eternal punishment"? "Not any longer," the voice of our King from Calvary answers. "It is finished. My blood cleanses you from all sin."

Talk about victory! Does an inner voice whisper to us, "You are a child of death, a sure victim of that king of terrors"? "Not any longer," the voice of our King from Calvary answers. "It is finished. I have abolished death and brought life and immortality."

Talk about victory! Does Satan still try to handcuff us to him in sin's slavery? "Not any longer," the voice of our King from Calvary answers. "It is finished. One little word can fell him."

But to talk about victory means to talk about the King. He did it! He is a King indeed! He is King of kings and Lord of lords!

Dear Savior, remind us ever of your Good Friday victory. Amen.

Now on his way to Jerusalem, Jesus traveled along the border between Samaria and Galilee. As he was going into a village, ten men who had leprosy met him. They stood at a distance and called out in a loud voice, "Jesus, Master, have pity on us!" (Luke 17:11-13)

ASK JESUS!

When trouble strikes, the natural reaction of man is to cry out for help. Men cry out to whatever they think will help them, be it someone in their family, or a doctor, or the government, or a god—someone stronger and wiser than themselves, someone to help in a need they cannot handle themselves.

But much of the time men cry out to what is unable to help them, to false gods, who do not exist, or to doctors and friends, who are limited in their wisdom and power. Much of the time, men cry out in vain.

We do not know how many times these ten lepers had cried out for help during the many years of their affliction with leprosy. Nor do we know whom they asked for help. We do know that no one did help them, for their leprosy continued and troubled them more with each passing year.

No one helped them—until they came to Jesus and asked Jesus to have mercy upon them. The measure of help is determined by the strength and ability of the helper. When all is said and done, there is only One who is powerful and able to help in every need. That is Jesus. He is the Son of God. He is true God from eternity to eternity. He has all wisdom and power in heaven and on earth.

As we hear of these lepers turning to Jesus for help, we remember that Jesus has invited all of us to bring our needs to him. And he has assured us that he will help us: "Call upon me in the day of trouble; I will deliver you, and you will honor me" (Psalm 50:15).

Days of trouble will come our way during our lives. Indeed, each day has enough sorrows of its own. In our need we cry out for help. And our help is in the name of the Lord. He made us, redeemed us, and will preserve us and all who call upon him unto his heavenly kingdom.

All that for my soul is needful
He with loving care provides,
Nor of that is He unheedful
Which my body needs besides.
In my need He doth not fail me.
All things else have but their day,
God's great love abides for aye. Amen.

As he was going into a village, ten men who had leprosy met him. They stood at a distance and called out in a loud voice, "Jesus, Master, have pity on us!" (Luke 17:12,13)

ASK JESUS IN ALL THE NEEDS OF LIFE

Leprosy was the common cancer in the days of the New Testament. Like cancer, leprosy was dreaded and feared. Like cancer, leprosy struck with no distinction of sex or age or previous health. Today cancer (and leprosy) can sometimes be treated, but 2,000 years ago there was no cure for leprosy. When a leper was detected, he was considered ceremonially unclean and sent away from his home and family; he was forbidden contact with society; he could not work but had to beg for his food and clothing; he could only suffer until his leprosy brought its own relief in death. Because lepers were so separated from other people, it is understandable that these ten lepers had banded together to aid and comfort one another in their hopeless situation.

Standing afar off, because they could not come close to those who did not have leprosy, the ten called out loudly to Jesus, that he might hear them and help them. They cried out to Jesus, for their need was great.

As those who know and trust Jesus, we also cry out to him in our needs. We needn't wait until we have a great need, for Jesus wants us to come to him in all the needs of life. He is not a helper only when things get to be "too much for us to handle." He is a helper for us in matters great and small, in every concern of life. No matter that we bring to Jesus is too small—or too great—for him.

He especially invites us to come to him to be cleansed of our leprosy—the leprosy of sin. Our sins have made us unclean and have separated us from God's fellowship. Our sins will bring us eternal death—unless they are cured. And we have a perfect cure in Christ, who shed his blood on the cross for us.

The invitation to come to Jesus is well expressed in one of our hymns:

Come in poverty and meanness,
Come defiled, without, within;
From infection and uncleanness,
From the leprosy of sin,
Wash your robes and make them white;
Ye shall walk with God in light.
(TLH 149:2)

Whatever our need, be it a need of the body or of the soul, Jesus always can help. And he always will help, for he is our Savior. He is our God.

Lord Jesus, have mercy upon us. Amen.

24

When he saw them, he said, "Go, show yourselves to the priests." (Luke 17:14)

ASK IN FAITH

J esus' answer to the ten lepers sounds strange to us. They had asked for healing, but Jesus said only, "Go, show yourselves to the priests." Though this answer puzzles us, the lepers understood it very well. The Old Testament regulations (in Leviticus 13 and 14) had a provision that priests were to serve as inspectors. They had the responsibility to certify that a person had leprosy and to certify it if a person were healed of leprosy. Jesus told these men to go to the priest so that he could pronounce them clean and welcome them back, as it were, into the "land of the living." In telling them to go to the priest, Jesus was promising them that they would be healed of their leprosy. This answer of Jesus to the ten lepers invited them to trust him. They had as of yet no physical indication of healing. They had only the promise of Jesus that they would be healed. By giving this kind of answer, Jesus sought to give the lepers a lesson in faith. He taught them to trust him as the Son of God and their Savior. They were to learn to trust him, not only for the healing of their bodies, but also, and especially, for the healing of their souls. They were to learn that in all their needs they could count on the help of Jesus.

We too have been given promises by Jesus. Like the lepers who heard this promise, we do not yet see the fulfillment of many of Jesus' promises to us. He has said that we are cleansed and purified from the leprosy of sin, but we still see sin in our lives. He has said that we have been delivered from death, but we still see the grave ahead of us. He has said that he is with us always, but none of us has ever seen Jesus face to face. He has said that we will see heaven, but all we see now is the pain and misery of this world.

In making such promises to us, Jesus is calling upon us to put our faith in him. As Jesus said, "Blessed are those who have not seen and yet have believed" (John 20:29). Blessed are we, who trust the promises Jesus has made to us. Blessed are we, who believe that he has cleansed our bodies of the leprosy of sin, that he has freed us from death, and that in him we have newness of life and immortality. Blessed are we, who believe the gospel of salvation. Blessed indeed! For all who believe it possess what it offers.

Our Father in heaven, we thank you for having brought us to faith in Jesus, your Son. Preserve our faith unto the end, for his sake. Amen.

Once more he visited Cana in Galilee, where he had turned the water into wine. And there was a certain royal official whose son lay sick at Capernaum. When this man heard that Jesus had arrived in Galilee from Judea, he went to him and begged him to come and heal his son, who was close to death. "Unless you people see miraculous signs and wonders," Jesus told him, "you will never believe." The royal official said, "Sir, come down before my child dies." Jesus replied, "You may go. Your son will live." The man took Jesus at his word and departed. (John 4:46-50)

LESS THAN WHAT HE ASKED FOR—AND MORE

A boy was sick. Help was badly needed. His father remembered Jesus. Faith sought the Lord. It made its plea. It asked Christ to come. And Jesus said no!

Or did he? It's true, Jesus didn't answer the father's prayer in the manner in which the father wanted him to answer it. And it was a good thing he didn't, for the father would have shorted himself. Jesus gave him less than what he asked for—and more!

The Lord gave the man less in that he did not accompany him to his house as he desired. In a manner of speaking, his request wasn't answered at all. Instead, the Lord gave the father a word of promise. He indicated that the lad would be healed, that if the father would simply return home he would find his petition granted. And this was the much greater gift, since it required faith on the part of the man to accept and believe the word of Jesus. He had faith in his heart already, or else he would not have sought out the Lord in the first place. Jesus' word of promise caused that faith to grow and become stronger. Don't you see that the Lord gave him much more than he asked for? When the man arrived home, not only was his son well, but he himself had been strengthened in his faith in the Savior.

There's a lesson in that for us. Whenever we go to the Lord in prayer, when we seek his assistance and help, let's never tie his almighty hands as this father almost did. We must learn to allow the Lord to answer our needs in the manner he thinks best. We would often shortchange ourselves. And when he answers our prayers in a way that is a bit different than we had anticipated, let's learn to look a bit more deeply, and we shall see that Jesus has granted us not less, but more, much more than we asked for. He knows much better than we do what we really need.

The father's strengthened faith is a fine example for our faith. Let us ever look for the word of promise our Savior gives us in Scripture, believe it, and trust in it. His promises give us all we need—and more!

Lord Jesus, grant me a faith that never doubts, but ever believes. As you answer my prayers, strengthen my faith to cling firmly to the promises of forgiveness and life eternal found in your glorious gospel. Amen.

A Canaanite woman from that vicinity came to him, crying out, "Lord, Son of David, have mercy on me! My daughter is suffering terribly from demon-possession." (Matthew 15:22)

LORD, I MUST TALK TO YOU!

The land of Syrophenicia began about 35 miles northwest of the Sea of Galilee. In Old Testament times the heathen Canaanite people fled to this valuable seacoast region to escape the children of Israel. This region was never subdued by God's chosen people. Tyre and Sidon—two famous commercial cities of the ancient world—were once located here. But long before the coming of Christ they had fallen under the wrath of God for their wicked, idolatrous ways and were completely destroyed.

But some of these heathen people had been exposed to the Jewish religion. They had heard of the Messiah who was to come to the Israelites. Nor were they ignorant of Jesus, whom many in neighboring Galilee believed to be this Messiah or Savior sent from God. When the Canaanite woman in our text heard of the miracles that Jesus was doing in Galilee and heard of his message concerning the kingdom of heaven, she was convinced that he was of God and could help her.

Tragedy and sadness had entered her home. The devil had taken possession of her daughter and made her life ugly and uncontrollable. Up to this point, life had seemed hopeless. Not that the woman hadn't sought help from her heathen religion. She had, but to no avail. Her gods were no gods. But in Jesus Christ lay hope. He not only claimed to be the Son of God who had come to save the people from their sins, but even did the works of God to prove it, including the casting out of devils. She had to talk to Jesus and ask his help!

But it wasn't only the POWER of Jesus that attracted her. It was also the COMPASSION. Jesus was easily touched with the feeling of sinful man's infirmities. Her former gods showed no compassion, but Jesus loved and pitied and helped people. She was convinced that her words of prayer would speak heart to heart and the Lord would help. She must talk to Jesus! Saving faith looks always to Jesus.

Jesus is our compassionate Lord and Savior. When our life is weary and sad; when we feel tempted by devil, world and flesh; when sickness strikes our body, or sin smites our conscience—whatever the need —let our heart cry, "Lord, I must talk to you!" Sinner, heart answers heart whenever we speak to Jesus. Only believe! Ever pray!

Lord, in all times of trial and need teach us to talk to you. Amen.

Jesus did not answer a word. (Matthew 15:23)

PATIENTLY WAIT FOR GOD'S ANSWER

"**J**esus did not answer a word." How strange the words sound! He did not say yes to her as we would expect. He did not say no. He just remained silent. Why? One reason was that Jesus was not sent to the Gentiles but to the Jewish people. But there is also another purpose for his silence. That was to teach her patience. The time was not exactly right for him to respond to her plea. He had heard it. He would answer. But he would do it when he knew it was best.

Does Jesus answer our prayers? This is a question which often faces the Christian. I know of old people who are suffering the pains of old age and long to die. They pray that the Lord will take them. Yet he remains silent. I know of people who pray for a healing, but it seems that the Lord is not hearing them; instead their disease continues to grow worse. I know of people who pray for a job where they can earn a decent living, but the days go by and there is no work or the pay is not enough. I know of students who pray for good grades and in spite of their diligent work continue to do poorly. I know of people who pray for their children who have fallen away from the church, but the pleas seem to go unanswered. Is Jesus hearing our prayers? Yes, Jesus is hearing our prayers. The problem is that we are not hearing the answer.

First of all, whenever we pray for spiritual blessings from Jesus, we can be sure that he gives us the answer in his Word. When we pray for the forgiveness of sins, he answers in his Word, "Your sins are forgiven." He has paid for all of them. When you pray for a strong faith, he answers that prayer through his Word and the Lord's Supper. He begins strengthening our faith immediately.

Secondly, whenever we pray for earthly or temporal blessings, he answers those prayers, but at his own time in the way that is best for us. Many times the things for which we pray would be harmful for us. We must learn that he knows what is best for our life so that we reach eternal life. Many times he delays the answer to our prayers to teach us patience. We are products of modern America, and as such we want instant satisfaction in everything. As Christians we must learn to be patient. May the Lord grant us patience as we wait for the answer we know the Lord will give.

Lord Jesus, teach us to pray with the certainty that our prayers are heard and answered. Give us the patience to wait for the answer that is best for our welfare now and forever. Amen.

The woman came and knelt before him. "Lord, help me!" she said. (Matthew 15:25)

JESUS INSTRUCTS US ABOUT PERSEVERANCE

"**I** quit. I give up." Very often this is our response when we try something for a while and it does not work out. But this is not to be our response when prayers seem to go unanswered.

Even though Jesus had told his disciples, "I was sent only to the lost sheep of Israel," the Canaanite woman did not give up in her efforts to have Jesus deliver her child from demon-possession. In fact it seems that this pause when Jesus spoke to his disciples gave the woman time to catch up with them. "She came and knelt before him." With all humility she bowed before her Lord. Her plea was, "Lord, help me." She still recognized Jesus as her Lord and only source of help for her daughter. She would not give up.

It would be interesting to know just what this woman had heard about Jesus. She must have heard of the way he healed all that were brought to him. Had she also heard of the teaching of Jesus, "All that the father gives me will come to me, and whoever comes to me I will never drive away" (John 6:37)? Had she heard the invitation of Jesus, "Come to me, all you who are weary and burdened, and I will give you rest" (Matthew 11:28)? We have no way of knowing the answers to these questions. What is important is that we learn from this woman to persevere in our faith in Jesus Christ.

We have a wealth of Scripture passages which show us that Jesus is able to do whatever we ask him. All of the miracles have been recorded for that purpose. We also know of the promises which he gave to his disciples. We know of his great invitation to come to him for rest. We have the examples of people in the Old Testament who were strong in their faith. We know how Abraham trusted that God would give him a child even though it seemed impossible. He persevered. We know how Jacob struggled with the Lord until the Lord blessed him. We know how the Lord listened to the pleading of Moses and spared the children of Israel.

Above all we know the love of the Lord Jesus for us. He was willing to come to earth, suffer and die for us. He was willing to take our place so that we might have eternal life. Because we know of his love toward us and that he also invites us to pray, we persevere in our faith in him.

Lord Jesus, when we hear your word, send your Holy Spirit into our hearts and work a faith which will persevere through all the trials of this life. Amen.

29

Then one of the synagogue rulers, named Jairus, came there. Seeing Jesus, he fell at his feet and pleaded earnestly with him, "My little daughter is dying. Please come and put your hands on her so that she will be healed and live." So Jesus went with him. (Mark 5:23,24)

TROUBLE UNDERNEATH—POWER UP ABOVE

When the sun shines and the breezes blow gently, the Sea of Galilee seems so peaceful. From the heights overlooking Tiberias one can observe sparkling waters and green hillsides sloping up from the lake. Appearances deceive. It is not always so calm. Some days there are strong winds, waves and danger.

Even so, many will still insist that Galilee is a delightful place to visit. An ideal place to vacation. So peaceful!

Jesus chose to live in a village in this area. The people of Galilee became his friends. He called some to be his witnesses. They would travel far and go to busy places. Could they ever forget this calm place?

But every peaceful scene may be the opposite underneath. Sin, trouble, sickness, despair and death emerge. All destroy peace. Wherever these are present—and this is everywhere—the quantity and quality of peace is limited.

Everything may have looked outwardly peaceful one day when Jesus discussed fasting with John's disciples. But several people had troubles that day. It took Jesus to restore peace. One home in Capernaum was far from peaceful. A little girl lay near death, the only daughter of the ruler of the synagogue. Peace disturbed by critical illness!

The death angel seemed close when the father, Jairus, went to Jesus with a simple request. When trouble finally disturbed his house, he felt that his neighbor, Jesus, had the power to help, as he had helped others.

The Savior's response? "Jesus went with him." So did the disciples. All went to where trouble underneath threatened to destroy Jairus's life.

No one lives in continual peace. Nothing grants immunity from occasional heartache. Where is help?

When trouble underneath disturbs our lives, Christians remember where the best help is—Jesus, through prayer. The centuries have not diminished his power to help. He can still rise from the right hand of power and come to our house when asked.

Dear Jesus, when there is trouble underneath, always be our power up above. Amen.

While Jesus was still speaking, someone came from the house of Jairus, the synagogue ruler. "Your daughter is dead," he said. "Don't bother the teacher any more." (Luke 8:49)

DONT BE AFRAID; JUST BELIEVE

The villagers of Capernaum had seen Jesus perform many miracles. A nobleman's son, a demoniac, Peter's mother-in-law, a palsied man and numerous invalids and cripples had felt the healing touch of the Great Physician. Fishermen had reported that the Sea of Galilee had calmed one night at Jesus' command. Yes, Jesus' neighbors experienced his power to heal and to control the elements.

But overcome death? That might be different. Who had done that since Elijah and Elisha? Did the friend who met Jairus returning home with Jesus think this?

Probably. The news he bears is bad. "Your daughter is dead; don't bother the teacher any more." A crushing message!

"Why did I wait so long before going to Jesus?" he may have thought. Or asked, "Why didn't Jesus come sooner?" Yes, no sense bothering Jesus now. A dear treasure, his one and only daughter is gone!

But the bruised reed, shocked and confused like most bereaved humans, is not broken off. Jesus' eye is on the broken father. He encourages, "Don't be afraid; just believe, and she will be healed."

How? The daughter was not sick anymore. She was dead! What could Jesus do about that?

Much, actually. Jesus can do much more about anything than even his children believe he can do. Short-sighted individuals forget that with God all things are possible. God's power is not limited. Jairus would have to trust that also.

How many hearts in trouble find it hard to hope like that? Many hesitant or qualified prayers seem to admit, "Jesus can do one thing but not another. I dare to ask for little but not for big things." So while they ask boldly for some things, they will not trouble the Master whenever the request seems like an impossible one.

Jesus does not scold Jairus's friends. Jairus is his concern. "Don't be afraid; just believe." That has to be enough for now. Jairus accepts. And waits. They continue on their way.

Tuck those words away in your hearts, believers! On our way through life remember that Jesus urges us also, "Don't be afraid; just believe." Even when the outlook seems completely hopeless and insurmountable, do not fear to trouble him further.

I know, Jesus, when my faith trusts you, you will honor my request for help. Amen.

He told her, "Go, call your husband and come back." "I have no husband," she replied. Jesus said to her, "You are right when you say you have no husband. The fact is, you have had five husbands, and the man you now have is not your husband. What you have just said is quite true." "Sir," the woman said, "I can see that you are a prophet." (John 4:16-19)

KNOWING ALL THEIR NEED

We are afraid to tell people what we need; sometimes even our friends. We are afraid they will laugh at us or hurt us. Or even worse that they will ignore us. Though this woman had some real problems, she had no one to talk to. Jesus showed her that he knew what she needed and that she could talk to him.

At first she did not say much; it was too painful. Her past had left deep scars on her heart. She had nothing to be proud of. She did not want to be reminded, though she needed to tell someone. Jesus understood. He showed her that he knew all about her. Nothing about any of us escapes his eye. He knows us just as we are. Because he loves us, he accepts us and forgives us.

He wants us to be open and honest with him. He invites us to pray to him, to lay all needs on him. As he says through Peter, "Cast all your anxiety on him because he cares for you." We may bring our big needs and our little ones, everything that is important to us. Jesus will not laugh at us or hurt us. He will do whatever is best for us. He will give us whatever is best for us.

He knows us better than we know ourselves. Because he is our good friend, he will help us with needs we are not even aware of. We are never left alone to struggle with our needs. Jesus sticks with us. He assures us, "I will never leave you nor forsake you." Everything will turn out for our good—that is his promise.

He can make such promises because he is the Lord of all creation. He makes everything we see, and he keeps it all running. He has the power to do what he promises; he earned it. He did everything his Father asked. With such willingness and love, he met our biggest need, our need to be forgiven. We have no reason to fear. Rather, "Let us then approach the throne of grace with confidence, so that we may receive mercy and find grace to help us in our time of need."

Dear Jesus, we hurt more than we can say. We have more needs than we know. But we are not afraid anymore, because we can tell you what we need. We know that you can help us in every need. We trust that you will help us and do what is best for us, because you have already loved us so much. Amen.

When they could not find a way to do this because of the crowd, they went up on the roof and lowered him on his mat through the tiles into the middle of the crowd, right in front of Jesus. (Luke 5:19)

BE PERSISTENT

How easily good intentions can evaporate when faced with a little resistance. We know how that works. A pastor intends to call on that member. But after several phone calls with no answer, and then no one home when he stops by, he lets that call wait until "later." A member intends to talk with his pastor. But when he finally gets up the courage to do so, there are too many people around, and he decides it wasn't that important. Think of how many sales have been lost, gardens not hoed, church services missed, because we let a little resistance stand in the way and don't persist.

God wants us to persevere in our faith, and in all that we ask for in faith. This is true, also, when we come to him for healing like these men did in our text. Did they say, "It's too crowded; no one will let us through with this stretcher; we'd better not bother Jesus when he's so busy; let's go home." No! They persisted. Faith finds a way. In this case, they moved back the movable tiles and went through the roof. They didn't give up until they had presented their case right in front of Jesus to let him decide what to do.

Jesus himself sets the best example of persistence for us. His human nature did not relish the thought of going any further in Gethsemane. Nevertheless he persisted in doing his Father's will and went all the way to Golgotha. And look at the blessings that resulted! Forgiveness for all our sins. Peace for our souls. Life with God forever in heaven. Jesus has given us spiritual healing and eternal good health because he persisted.

When it comes to seeking out Jesus also for earthly blessings—including healing—God wants us to be persistent. Remember the Syrophoenician woman and her crumbs? God hasn't promised always to heal us in the way we want it or according to our timetable. Sometimes he says, "My grace is sufficient for you." But he also says, "You do not have, because you do not ask God." He says we "should always pray and not give up." Be persistent. It may not seem like you can find a way at first. But persevere in faith to bring all your needs right in front of Jesus. And let him decide.

Dear Jesus, sometimes I get discouraged in my faith. Help me to be persistent in bringing all my needs to you until you meet them in your way. Amen.

Jesus said, "Have the people sit down." There was plenty of grass in that place, and the men sat down, about five thousand of them. Jesus then took the loaves, gave thanks, and distributed to those who were seated as much as they wanted. He did the same with the fish. (John 6:10,11)

PRAYER—BAROMETER OF FAITH

A barometer is an instrument which measures air pressure. When the pressure is high and steady, then the sky is clear, the sun shines, and the weather is enjoyable. When the barometer drops, it indicates that there is going to be a change in the weather. When the weather is unstable, the sky is probably cloudy, and there is a threat of severe storms.

Our prayer-life serves as a barometer of our Christian faith. Prayer does not create faith any more than a barometer causes the weather. But prayer is an accurate gauge and measure of the strength of our faith. If it reads high, if we are praying a lot, it is an indication that our faith is strong and that our hearts are unclouded. If the barometer is low, if we pray little or not at all, we may well take that as a sign that our faith is growing weak and expect storm clouds to appear on the horizon.

Before Jesus had his disciples distribute the bread and fish to the hungry people who had followed him, he prayed. Jesus' prayer is an example to every believing heart. By his prayer Jesus showed that the blessing of food which was to follow was a gift from God. His prayer of thanks was his way of professing that God deserves the credit for providing our food, drink, clothing, shelter, family, friends, good weather, good health and all that we need for our body and life.

When we give thanks to God for our daily bread it is an evidence of faith. For our prayer of gratitude acknowledges the Creator's love and ability to preserve our life. It flows from our knowledge of our Redeemer's sacrificial love. And it is a product of the Comforter's work of having brought us to faith in Jesus. According to that faith, let us daily join the psalmist, who experienced God's gracious providence, and foresaw and believed his promises in Christ. He prayed: "Give thanks to the Lord, for he is good; his love endures forever."

Oh, may we ne'er with thankless heart
Forget from whom our blessings flow!
Still, Lord, Thy heav'nly grace impart;
Still teach us what to Thee we owe.
Lord, may our lives with fruit divine
Return Thy care and prove us Thine. Amen.

Deliver us from evil. (Luke 11:4)

THE LORD TURNS EVIL INTO GOOD

Only the very inexperienced are surprised when something breaks, fails to function, or goes wrong. The older you get the more you realize that sooner or later everything in the world wears out, clogs up, rusts, becomes diseased, withers, rots, dies or becomes useless. This is the disastrous result of sin. Sin covers creation like dew. Nothing escapes. Everything is affected. Everything is doomed.

When you think about the world covered with the curse of sin, you almost want to yell out, "Get me out of here!" God will, in due time, get us out of this vale of tears. But in the mean time we should cherish our life as priceless. Our life is God's gift. Eternal life is his greater gift. True, we are still in an evil world, but we will overcome. "He who overcomes will inherit all this, and I will be his God and he will be my son" (Revelation 21:17).

While we trudge through this sin-cursed world we pray, "Lord, deliver us from evil." We don't expect to be engulfed in a pink cloud and be spared all the agonies, disappointments and heartaches of life. Evil is part of life.

When we pray "Deliver us from evil," we pray that God in his good pleasure might turn some of that evil into good as he turned the hatred of Joseph's eleven brothers into the good of raising Joseph to the position of leadership in Egypt, or as the Lord strengthened Job through affliction.

My favorite comfort passage at the bedside of a down-hearted Christian is Romans 8:28, "And we know that in all things God works for the good of those who love him, who have been called according to his purpose."

God can and does turn the evil of life into great blessings for his children. The other evening my wife and I were together with three Christian couples. Two couples had already buried one of their children; the other couple is raising a handicapped daughter. But these are devout and contented people because they are in Christ and they have learned to glory even in their tribulation.

We pray in this petition, as the sum of all, that our Father in heaven would deliver us from every evil of body and soul, of property and honor, and finally, when our last hour shall come, grant us a blessed end, and graciously take us from this vale of tears to himself In heaven. Amen.

Jesus, knowing that they intended to come and make him king by force, withdrew again to a mountain by himself. (John 6:15)

GOD GIVES US WHAT WE REALLY NEED

Would you like to be able to command God to do just what you want him to do in your life? Would you like him to give you a blank check on which you could fill in any desired amount? Jesus knew what these people wanted from him—even before they asked. And he refused their request for their own good.

When the crowd realized that Jesus was able to perform miracles, they wanted to make the most of his presence in their midst. They wanted him to be their king and free them from the oppression of the Roman authorities. They wanted Jesus to provide for all their needs with no effort on their part. They wanted him to be their bread king.

Jesus had something much better in mind for them. He would let them continue to live with the responsibilities that God had given them in this life. But he would gain eternal life for them, so that they might have permanent happiness and freedom from cares in the life to come. Those were much greater blessings than any earthly king could provide for them.

When Jesus satisfied the demands of God's justice on the cross, he was not suffering judgment for his own sins. He was dying for the sins of all the people. He took God's anger over our sins upon himself, that we might bask in God's favor and love for all of time and eternity. He died that we might live forevermore.

Beyond that, he rose that we might rise to life eternal at the last day, as well as have life in him now. In all these ways he showed that he really cares for us. He would not let this eager crowd turn him from his love-wrought purpose. He withdrew from them, because he wanted to do what was really good for them. He went to give his life in their place.

We can be happy that when we pray to God, he does not always give us exactly what we want. We may pray for all good things that we desire, but we often do not understand what would really be good for us. But God knows all things. He knows what is best for us, and that is what he gives us. "We do not know what we ought to pray, but the Spirit himself intercedes for us with groans that words cannot express." In this way God gives us what is really good for us.

Dear Jesus, I thank you that you care for me. Thank you for giving me the best gift of all, the everlasting salvation purchased with your precious blood and your innocent suffering and death. In your name I pray. Amen.

"Take my yoke upon you and learn from me, for I am gentle and humble in heart, and you will find rest for your souls. For my yoke is easy and my burden is light." (Matthew 11:29-30)

"COME UNTO ME YE WEARY"

"Come unto Me, ye weary, and I will give you rest" is one of those hymns that strikes the chords of joyous melody in our hearts, and well it might. For it comes to those whose hearts are oppressed and promises them "pardon, grace and peace—of joy that hath no ending, of love which cannot cease." To the wanderers, to those whose hearts are filled with sadness, it promises "gladness and songs at break of day." To those who are "fainting" it promises life; to those engaged in a fierce struggle against Satan it promises strength to win the victory.

Christ continually invites us to leave our heavy burden of sin and shame on his shoulders and in return to accept a light burden from him. Those who leave their heavy burden of sin with Christ, are not going to be without a burden altogether. Christ will give them another in its place, a light burden though, one that is actually a privilege. It is the yoke of the cross, which Christians must be prepared to bear in this world as disciples of him who first bore the cross for us. Though the heavy burden of sin has been lifted, there will still be trials and tribulations, for the disciple is not above his master. This burden will prove irksome to our flesh.

And yet, compared with the heavy burden of sin which has been lifted from us, the yoke of Christ is easy and his burden is light. The Christian knows that these crosses do not come upon him by chance or accident. They are sent into his life by a loving God and are intended for his good. The Christian also knows that God will never let the cross become heavier than he is able to bear. With each trial of faith God will also provide the ability to endure. God will supply the necessary strength for each new day. Hence, the burden of Christ, far from separating us from the love of God, will only draw us much closer to him. The affliction of the body will be turned to the eternal good of our soul.

Whenever we are crushed by the heavy burden of sin, or when we become anxious and troubled by the problems that we face in a world of sin, let us immediately go to the right place, to him who graciously tells us:

And whosoever cometh,
I will not cast him out.
O patient love of Jesus,
Which drives away our doubt,
Which, tho' we be unworthy
Of love so great and free,
Invites us very sinners
To come dear Lord to Thee. Amen.

37

Then Jesus went up on the hillside and sat down with his disciples. The Jewish Passover Feast was near. When Jesus looked up and saw a great crowd coming toward him, he said to Philip, "Where shall we buy bread for these people to eat?" He asked this only to test him, for he already had in mind what he was going to do. (John 6:3-6)

TESTS FOR DISCIPLES

Giving a test still seems to be one of the best ways for a teacher to gauge the progress of his pupils. Throughout our lives we are required to pass various kinds of tests to determine our level of achievement. We must pass a driver's license examination in order to use the highways. Various types of psychological and aptitude testing are done by companies in connection with the employment and advancement of their workers.

When a multitude of people followed Jesus around the Sea of Galilee, Jesus gave a test to his student, his disciple Philip. He asked him, "How can we buy enough bread to feed all those people?" The test which Jesus gave, however, was not like those which an ordinary teacher might give to his pupils. Because Jesus was the Son of God, he already knew everything there was to know about Philip. He knew how strong Philip's faith was. He knew what Philip was thinking when he saw a multitude of people coming to Jesus. Jesus' test of Philip was not to determine Philip's aptitude or ability. Jesus was testing or trying Philip's faith so that it might become stronger.

God tests all Christians in this same way. He tests our faith to make it stronger. He exercises our faith by allowing questions and problems to enter into our daily lives. His purpose is not to hurt us, but to strengthen us. "God is faithful; he will not let you be tempted beyond what you can bear. But when you are tempted, he will also provide a way out so that you can stand up under it."

This is a comforting thought for us, who are tempted by Satan to doubt God's love and to question his purposes in the midst of suffering. God promises that, for Jesus' sake, he will allow his people to suffer only for their good. It is true that "no discipline seems pleasant at the time, but painful. Later on, however, it produces a harvest of righteousness and peace for those who have been trained by it."

**From dark temptation's power,
From Satan's wiles, defend.
Deliver in the evil hour
And guide us to the end. Amen.**

When Jesus looked up and saw a great crowd coming toward him, he said to Philip, "Where shall we buy bread for these people to eat?" He asked this only to test him, for he already had in mind what he was going to do. Philip answered him, "Eight months' wages would not buy enough bread for each one to have a bite!" Another of his disciples, Andrew, Simon Peter's brother, spoke up, "Here is a boy with five small barley loaves and two small fish, but how far will they go among so many?" (John 6:5-9)

HE GENTLY BRINGS OUT FAITH

There are times when we feel there is nowhere to turn. We feel trapped. Philip could see no way out of the predicament the people were in. It was impossible for Philip to buy food for them because there was not enough money available.

There are times when we don't have enough money to take care of all our expenses. We may get desperate. Perhaps we look for a second income, or we go deeper into debt. Sooner or later we have to tighten our belts and lower our standard of living until we earn our way out. But in the meantime we may frantically enter every sweepstakes or contest that comes in the mail, or we may waste our meager resources on lottery tickets. We may even rely on such things rather than trusting in God to provide.

Philip did not know where to get food for all the people. So Jesus asked a question to test him. He wanted Philip to be aware of his own inadequacies, and then he wanted Philip to look to his Savior for the solution for this pressing problem.

Jesus is right beside us all the time, too. We need to place our cares and our worries into his hands. "Cast all your anxiety on him because he cares for you." He is strong enough and wise enough to make everything turn out right.

It is difficult for us to trust God to take care of all our problems. Perhaps we feel he takes care of our spiritual problems, our sins, but we are responsible for our physical needs. He invites us to cast all our cares upon him, for he cares for us, and "we know that in all things God works for the good of those who love him, who have been called according to his purpose."

Lord Jesus, help me to realize every time a problem comes into my life that you care for me and you will provide the right solution in the proper time. I place my life into your hands. Amen.

When they had all had enough to eat, he said to his disciples, "Gather the pieces that are left over. Let nothing be wasted." So they gathered them and filled twelve baskets with pieces of the five barley loaves left over by those who had eaten. (John 6:12,13)

GOD KNOWS OUR NEEDS

Worry is a sin against the First Commandment. The First Commandment requires an absolute trust in God and his promises to provide for us. Worry and consternation are the very opposite of trust and confidence in God. Worry suggests that God is unconcerned about his people, unwilling to help them or perhaps even unable to do so. Among Jesus' disciples there had been much concern, if not worry, about the five thousand men who were without food on the eastern shores of the Sea of Galilee. Philip pointed out that there was not enough money to buy food. Andrew looked at the loaves that were available and said, "But how far will they go among so many?"

Have we ever been guilty of sinful worrying, as though God were incapable of handling our situation? In his "Sermon on the Mount" Jesus told us not to worry. He said, "So do not worry, saying, 'What shall we eat?' or 'What shall we drink?' or 'What shall we wear?' For the pagans run after all these things, and your heavenly Father knows that you need them."

When he fed the five thousand, Jesus demonstrated the heavenly Father's attention to our daily needs. Not only did God provide, but he provided so much and so well that they needed twelve baskets to gather the food that remained. So we are daily led to an appreciation of God's great love when we see how he provides for us in spite of our worry and far beyond that which we even have time to request.

But this should come as no surprise. For God showed his love a long time ago in a way much more generous than anyone ever could have imagined. How can we worry when we know by faith what great love he first demonstrated by sending Jesus to be our Savior! "For God so loved the world that he gave his one and only Son, that whoever believes in him shall not perish but have eternal life." In Christ, God has taken care of the greatest and most vital needs of our souls. How then can we think for a moment that he cannot see or provide the lesser, namely, what we need for our daily, bodily life!

Yes, God gives daily bread indeed without our asking, even to all the wicked; but we pray that he would lead us to receive ours with thankful appreciation.

Our Father in heaven, give us this day our daily bread, and lead us to receive it every day with gratitude in Jesus' name. Amen.

He looked up to heaven and with a deep sigh said to him, "Ephphatha!" (which means, "Be opened!"). (Mark 7:34)

THE LORD'S CONCERN FOR THE INDIVIDUAL

People communicate very effectively with sounds other than words. For example, a parents' gasp says that their daredevil two-year-old has struck again. An executive's deep sigh signifies a hard day at the office. The cheers of the crowd give approval to the home team. Sounds that people make are significant, even if many of them are not real words.

Our Lord Jesus was a master communicator. He could express himself not only with words but also with other sounds. We notice one sound, a sympathetic sigh, in the Scripture verse above.

As Jesus looked at the man standing in front of him, unable to speak and unable to hear, he could not but pity him. Here was a human being, whose ancestor, Adam, had been created perfectly in God's own image and yet upon whom human sinfulness had taken its physical and spiritual toll. Jesus sighed because in this man he saw the pitiful condition typical of all people, for all are heirs of Adam's sinful nature and are guilty of many sinful deeds of their own.

Jesus healed many people day after day, but none of his healings were just impersonal demonstrations of his power. Our Lord took a personal interest in every person who came or was brought to him for healing. His sigh shows his concern for this individual.

Take Jesus' sigh as a sign to you that he is also concerned about you and all your troubles. He has experienced everything that you can imagine. Are you hurting because you have lost a loved one? Jesus knows what that is like. Are you fighting against a repeated temptation which seems more difficult to resist each time? Jesus can sympathize with you. Are you tired of carrying your own problems as well as those of others? Jesus sighs with you. You are not alone. Anything you experience Jesus has gone through too, but without sin.

The sympathetic sigh of your Savior also tells you that Jesus had an earnest desire to help, and help he did. What greater burden could you bring to God than the burden of your sins and their sentence of death? Yet Jesus was so sympathetic toward you that he carried your sins and the burden of your debt on his own shoulders. He sympathized with you to the point of giving his life to pay off what you could not pay—the debt of all your sins.

You are never alone. Jesus is always present with you. He sympathizes with you in all your problems and temptations. He provides the only solution to the disaster of sin. Lean on and trust in him. He is your sympathetic Savior.

Lord, thank you for the comfort of your sympathy. Amen.

He looked up to heaven and with a deep sigh said to him, "Ephphatha!" (which means, "Be opened!"). At this, the man's ears were opened, his tongue was loosened and he began to speak plainly. (Mark 7:34,35)

THE WONDERFUL WORD OF POWER

T.G.I.F. Some weeks are so hectic and tiresome that people have coined the phrase, "Thank God It's Friday!" After a week of work and other activities we may welcome the weekend as a time to regain some lost energy. Where will you look this weekend to recharge yourself? Where will you look for help today?

Jesus used something very powerful to heal this man. It was not a special potion. It was not a prescription drug. The power to heal lay in Jesus' almighty word. He simply said, "Be opened!" and the man's ears and tongue were healed. When we think of words of power, we are reminded of the creation account in Genesis 1. The psalmist writes, "By the word of the LORD were the heavens made." For the man who was deaf and mute, Jesus' word was also filled with God's power.

Jesus' word is still powerful to heal. St. Paul calls the Word of God and especially the good news of Jesus "the power of God for the salvation of everyone who believes." Without the Word we would not come to know of Jesus. Without the Word we could not believe in Jesus. Without the Word we could not be forgiven. With the Word all this and much, much more is accomplished. Jesus' word is the power of God which brings us to faith and salvation in Jesus Christ.

We can consult God's Word for other reasons also. Do you need guidance for your life? Do you need to have your energy level recharged? Get in touch with the gospel of Jesus in his Word, in baptism and in the Lord's Supper. Familiarize yourself with all God's promises to you for now and for eternity, and be filled with enthusiasm and energy from God.

When you feel drained of your energy, the only thing that helps is rest. Jesus promises that, if we come to him wearied and burdened, he will give us the ultimate in rest—rest for our souls. Get into the habit of enjoying such rest daily through his wonderful word of power, and thank God for opportunities to serve him with gladness every day of the week.

Almighty God, by your Word give us strength and energy for each new day. Amen.

When he had finished speaking, he said to Simon, "Put out into deep water, and let down the nets for a catch." Simon answered, "Master, we've worked hard all night and haven't caught anything. But because you say so, I will let down the nets." When they had done so, they caught such a large number of fish that their nets began to break. (Luke 5:4-6)

FAITH IS ALWAYS HONORED

Are you kidding, Lord? Fish aren't caught in deep water. Besides, we have been trying all night. I don't think we had better do this. We'll make fools of ourselves and everyone will laugh at us. Are you absolutely sure that this is what you want us to do?

Yes, Peter could have made such statements in answer to the Lord's command. Might not we have answered in much the same way? But Peter didn't. He believed Jesus' words. And faith was honored!

If this were a principle that is new, a principle not found elsewhere in the Scriptures, we might not give it a great deal of attention. But it happens to be a principle that is repeated in nearly every chapter of the Bible. Faith which believes the Word is always honored. Never, let me repeat, never, has our God failed to make good on a promise which he has asked us to accept in faith. Now, that's a claim no one else can make for himself. Our best friends, the most trusted members of our family circle, our most dependable acquaintances cannot say that they have never failed us, that they have never gone back on their word. Neither can we. But God can!

That's why it is so imperative that we believe the Word of our God. All his promises concerning our physical well-being here on earth are promises he will keep. And far more important, all his promises concerning our spiritual well-being, both now and for eternity, will come to pass. Because of what his Son did for us on Calvary's cross, our God can say to us, "You are mine." And we can trust that the relationship which is ours through the forgiveness purchased by our Savior is a relationship which has everlasting implications. It is not a relationship which will dim with time, as so many earthly friendships do. Rather, it is something that has substance.

The writer to the Hebrews says of faith, "Now faith is the substance of things hoped for, the evidence of things not seen." God keeps his promises. They are for real. By faith we know that God will keep them, just as surely as Peter found the fish in his net.

O Holy Spirit, overcome my doubts and allow faith to take over in my heart. May I believe your Word, and through such believing enter the mansions above! Amen.

Some men came carrying a paralytic on a mat and tried to take him into the house to lay him before Jesus. (Luke 5:18)

BASE YOUR HOPE ON JESUS

Good health is one of God's best earthly blessings. When we don't have it, we really miss it. When we do have it, we should appreciate it and remember to praise God for it.

Unfortunately, good health is not automatic in this world of sin. The healthy young athlete may take for granted his ability to race down the sideline under a pass, or circle the bases on a long line drive. But when he's confined to a wheelchair following a car accident, then what wouldn't he give not to be paralyzed? Is there any hope he'll walk again?

The answer to that question lies in the hands of the same person to whom some men carried a paralytic in our text. They came to the house where Jesus was and sought to lay their friend before him. They based their hope for help on Jesus.

What about you? Maybe you are one who is reading this devotion on your back in a hospital bed. Maybe it is your loved one awaiting lab tests on a tumor. What are your hopes for recovery? Do what these men did. Base your hopes on Jesus and lay your needs before him. Yes, go to that cardiologist if your doctor feels it would be helpful to call in a heart specialist. Yes, make that appointment at the Mayo Clinic if your medical needs require it. Doctors and hospitals are among the natural means that God has given to help provide for our earthly lives.

But, above all else, look to Jesus. Like the tearful child who brings the broken bike to his father and lays it before him for fixing; like the fearful mother who brings her feverish infant to the doctor and lays it before him for healing, so, first and foremost, we should bring all our needs to the Lord and lay them before him. "Cast all your anxiety on him because he cares for you."

Jesus does care for you. He cared enough to suffer for your sins. He cared enough to endure hell for you on the cross, to die, in order to fix your broken life and heal your sinsick soul. If he cared that much for you, do you not think he will care about your earthly needs also, whether they are emotional, or medical, or financial or anything?

Trust him. We do not know whether he has healing in store for our earthly lives. But we do know he loves us. We know he hears our prayers and will bring to pass what he knows is best for us. And we can't ask for anything better than that. Base your hopes on him.

Lord, help me to look to you for healing, and for everything. Amen.

Jesus knew what they were thinking and asked, "Why are you thinking these things In your hearts? Which is easier: to say, 'Your sins are forgiven,' or to say, 'Get up and walk'? But that you may know that the Son of Man has authority on earth to forgive sins. . . ." He said to the paralyzed man, "I tell you, get up, take your mat and go home." (Luke 5:22-24)

GOOD REASON TO HOPE

Hopeless! Sometimes that's the way we feel about things. My doctor says there is nothing more he can do for me, and I don't have any hope for getting better. My feelings tell me I have sinned too greatly for God to forgive me, and I feel my situation is hopeless.

But that's our human nature speaking. Let faith prevail! Listen to the words that Jesus speaks and let them assure you that our situation is never hopeless. With Jesus as our God we have good reason to hope.

Look at the assurance in our text. Some skeptical religious scholars privately doubted that Jesus had the authority to forgive sins. That was an amazing contradiction in itself. They apparently were willing to concede that Jesus could perform miracles of healing. The evidence of that was all over Galilee. But they didn't think Jesus was God and could forgive sins. Sometimes we reverse their doubts. We are willing to concede that Jesus is God and forgives our sins, and then we begin to doubt that Jesus cares about us enough, or has the ability, to heal our bodies.

To this Jesus says, "I know what you are thinking. Why do you doubt me? Which is easier to do, forgive sins or heal diseases?" Only God can do either one. Only God can forgive sins, though he may use ministers and other spokesmen in the church to pronounce that forgiveness. And only God can heal bodies, though he may use medicines and doctors to accomplish that end. To prove his authority, as God, to forgive sins, Jesus said to the paralyzed man, "Get up and walk."

Here is our reason for hope. With God nothing is impossible. Who can take a shriveled limb and, without surgery or therapy, make it whole? No miracle drug, only God himself. Who can take terminally ill souls and with the balm of his grace heal us of our sins and give us eternal life? No mere man, only the God-man.

God has not promised that he will always heal our bodies the way we desire. But he has promised to care for our earthly lives as a loving Father and give us what is best for our faith—without exception. He has promised that where his church is, he, too, is present with the forgiveness of sins and all his blessings. And what God says, he does. We have every reason to hope.

Dear Lord Jesus, help me always to place my hope in you. Amen.

Immediately he stood up in front of them, took what he had been lying on and went home praising God. (Luke 5:25)

HOPE IS REWARDED

The paralyzed man is healed! His faith, and that of his friends, was rewarded. Their prayers were granted. The skeptics were silenced. What telling testimony to the truth that those who place their hope in God are not disappointed.

There are two kinds of healing that people require. There is healing of the body, which we all need at times. For it is a rare person who at age eighty can say that he has never been to the doctor's office or spent a day in bed with the flu. And there is healing of the soul, which we all need at all times. For there is no one born who is without sin. For both kinds of healing we can turn to our Lord in hope and trust that he will help us.

The paralyzed man in our text had his hope rewarded. His concerns over sin were dispelled when Jesus forgave him his sins. And his desire for bodily health was granted when Jesus told him to get up. And he did. No assistance was needed to steady him. No weak muscles needed to be strengthened. There was no lengthy period of rehabilitation. "Immediately" he stood up and was able to carry home the stretcher that had carried him there.

God will not disappoint our hopes in him either. He may not give us immediate recovery from illness or accident. In fact, in most cases the healing process he gives us involves things like walkers and I-Vs. But whether we "miraculously" recover as one on whom the doctors had given up hope, or chronically continue on, we "know that in all things God works for the good of those who love him." Our faith and hope in God will not be disappointed.

With the healing of our souls, on the other hand, our recovery is always immediate and complete. No delays. No partial forgiveness. When we turn in repentance and faith to our God for help, we rejoice in the fact that he has already healed us. "If we confess our sins, he is faithful and just and will forgive us our sins and purify us from all unrighteousness." We will not have to suffer or die for our sins, because Christ already suffered and died for us— 2,000 years ago. Our hope in him will never be disappointed.

One more thing. Do not forget what the formerly paralyzed man did on his way home. He "went home praising God." Hopes that are realized lead to happiness and thankfulness. In your homes, in your hymns and in your hearts remember always to praise the God of your salvation.

I praise you with my whole heart, O God, for all your goodness to me. Amen.

Say in a word, and my servant shall be healed. (Luke 7:7)

CONFIDENT FAITH

What is a man's word worth today? Nothing gripes this writer more than empty promises made by repairmen, contractors, salesmen, or, for that matter, friends.

"It will be done tomorrow," he says.

You take him at his word. You drive the distance to his shop only to hear, "It's not ready yet." And you come to the bitter conclusion that you were only being strung along.

You and I do not like being strung along by anyone for any length of time. And we have been "taken" so often by the business world and by friends (I use that word "friends" quite loosely). Therefore we might fault God for stringing us along with something that is very important with us, such as: Will our sick dear one get better? Will I grow in faith? Will I carry out my desire to be a better Christian?

We make our request known in prayer to our Lord on Sunday morning and expect an answer by Sunday afternoon. And when it takes a while for us to see God's answer to our prayers in our life, we might accuse him of stringing us along.

So I will rephrase the initial question. What is God's Word worth today? Can it be taken to mean something? Will God's promise mean action in my life?

Jesus simply had to speak the word, and the centurion's servant would be healed. That is what the centurion believed, and it was enough for him. And if Jesus chose to carry out his request in miracle form in that way, that is the way it would be done.

When we take our broken hearts, lives and souls to the Repairman from Nazareth, results are guaranteed. They will be long lasting because Jesus is God. He has earned our salvation by his death on Calvary's cross. He is also our Good Shepherd.

We won't be put off with our problems when we go to Jesus for a solution. We won't be put down because our names do not carry any weight. Jesus knows us by name. Nor will we be put to the bottom of the list. Jesus plays no favorites.

Jesus' word means action in our life. Action now . . . for now and eternity.

O Lord, I wait patiently for your answer. I am confident that it is already on the way for Jesus' sake. Amen.

When Jesus had again crossed over by boat to the other side of the lake, a large crowd gathered around him while he was by the lake. Then one of the synagogue rulers, named Jairus, came there. Seeing Jesus, he fell at his feet and pleaded earnestly with him, "My little daughter is dying. Please come and put your hands on her so that she will be healed and live." (Mark 5:21-23)

DESPERATION

St. Mark will tell us later that Jairus's daughter was twelve years old. St. Luke adds that she was "his only daughter." We aren't told what disease she had. But it doesn't really matter, does it? The one thing that mattered most of all to Jairus was that his little girl's life was slowly slipping away. And there didn't seem to be much of anything he could do about it. Helplessness gradually gave way to desperation. He had to do something.

It was hard to walk out of the house. For all he knew, by the time he could get back to her, his little girl would be dead. And if she had to die, he certainly wanted to be there as she drew her last breath. But as hard as it was to leave, it would have been even harder to stay and wait for the inevitable without doing anything to try to help her.

Jairus had to do something, but he didn't know if he would be able to find Jesus. Perhaps Jesus was not even in Capernaum at the moment. He had recently crossed over to the other side of the Sea of Galilee to visit the region of the Gadarenes.

Jairus had no way of knowing when Jesus would return. But how could he ever forgive himself if he were to let his daughter die without even trying to locate Jesus?

With a sense of desperation, Jairus left his wife with his dying daughter and headed down toward the water, and once again we see God performing one of his almost invisible miracles of timing. It was more than a coincidence that Jesus' boat had just landed and "a large crowd gathered around him while he was by the lake." He was easy to find.

Everyone wanted to get close to Jesus, but maybe they recognized Jairus as "one of the synagogue rulers" and let him through out of respect for his office. And no doubt they could see the desperation on his face and in his movements as he made his way through the crowd and fell at Jesus' feet to beg for help.

Desperate people don't always think clearly, but in Jairus we see an example worthy of imitation. When you are feeling desperate, go and find Jesus and fall at his feet. He will not disappoint you.

Lord, please lay your hands on me so that I may live. Amen.

"Every branch that does bear fruit he prunes so that it will be even more fruitful." (John 15:2)

PRUNED BRANCHES

"God doesn't love me anymore!" Sometimes we feel this way when we are experiencing suffering and adversity. We make this mistake because we tend to equate love exclusively with blessing and happiness. We must learn not to pity ourselves when we are experiencing God's chastening. Remember, you and I are branches of God's vine. He is trimming us to make us useful. He must either prune us or sever us.

This is not to say that pruning is not painful. It is only to say that pruning is better than being "cut off." Anything is better than to have God abandon us in this life to the wiles of the devil and in the hereafter to the horrors of hell. Trust God to remove from your life what he knows would hurt you.

A man visiting a chrysanthemum show stood amazed at the beautiful blossoms. He noted the wide variety of colors and forms, but was impressed most of all by their size. "How do you produce such marvelous blooms?" he asked one of the gardeners. "We concentrate the strength of the plant on just one or two blossoms," the gardener replied. "If we allowed the plant to bear all the flowers it would like to, none of them would be worth showing. If we are to have a prize-winning plant, we must be content with one or two blossoms instead of a dozen."

This gardener described the way God works. In order to help us grow more like him, he cuts away the useless shoots of pride, greed or lust, so that we have singleness of purpose. He also uses his pruning knife to teach us that we cannot sin with impunity. Though we are not punished for our sins as unbelievers are, yet the consequences of our sins are often visited upon us, and thus we come to understand the heinousness of sin in God's sight. As we allow God to prune away the things harmful to our spiritual lives, our faith is strengthened until we become "more fruitful" branches fit for the gardens of eternity.

Remember, pruning is not punishment. Thanks be to God, Jesus has borne that. If sometimes we suffer under God's knife, let's try to imagine how we would agonize under his wrath, and then let's thank our Savior anew for enduring that wrath for us. God's pruning is never done in wrath. "The Lord disciplines those he loves."

O loving heavenly Father, when you send chastisements, help us to bear them and benefit from them and be comforted in your love. We pray in our Savior's name. Amen.

When the Counselor comes, whom I will send to you from the Father, . . . he will tesify about me. (John 15:26)

SOMEONE TO COMFORT YOU

In India, along the winding roads, especially in the hill countries, there are little resting places for travelers. They are similar to our waysides in appearance, and they are called "samatanga." Here a person may rest his weary feet, lay down his burden, and pause to talk with other travelers like himself. Then, rested, refreshed and encouraged, he may resume his journey.

How well we could use such places of rest as we travel the road called life! Along the way we encounter and must shoulder many sorrows which weigh us down. We grieve over the loved ones who have passed into the Lord's presence, leaving an empty place in our lives which no one else can fill. We wrestle with discouraging and painful personal and family problems which seem to gnaw away at our hearts night and day, robbing us of peace and joy in life. We fall to our knees under the crosses which our Lord in his wisdom allows us to bear from time to time. We grow weary under the burden of our guilt and sins. How we long for a spiritual "samatanga," a place where we can find a moment's peace, breathe a sigh of relief, find at least some refreshment for our souls.

Our Lord has provided us with just such a place. You know where it is— at the foot of the cross of Jesus. There we find the assurance that all is well between God and us, no matter how rough the road of life might become. And in case we have trouble finding this place when we need it and, blinded by grief and sorrow, should lose our way, Jesus has sent his Comforter, the Holy Ghost, to be our guide. It is this Comforter who takes us by the hand and leads us back to Calvary. There we are reminded that God is no longer angry with us, that he poured out on his Son the wrath we deserved. There he gave us righteousness, and hope, and life. And no man or devil can take it away from us!

So if the cares and worries of life are threatening to overwhelm you; if you feel yourself sinking under a tremendous load, then go back to the promises of God in Christ. For in them you will find not only a passing "samatanga," but eternal rest and comfort for your souls.

Come, Holy Ghost, in love
Shed on us from above
Thine own bright ray.
Divinely good Thou art.
Thy sacred gifts impart
To gladden each sad heart.
Oh, come today! Amen.

So he came to a town in Samaria called Sychar, near the plot of ground Jacob had given to his son Joseph. Jacob's well was there, and Jesus, tired as he was from the journey, sat down by the well. It was about the sixth hour. (John 4:5,6)

THE MIRACLE OF GOD'S LOVE

After a bitter argument between friends, a husband and wife, or brothers and sisters, someone has to make the move, the first move to bring them back together. It works best if the one who did the hurting or began the trouble, makes that first move. How hard it is! But how necessary, if things are to be healed. Only love enables us to rise above our hurt and pride to forgive and to ask forgiveness.

Here is the miracle of God's love. Though he has been offended, and ignored, and denied, he makes the first move. We can only run away and hide. We sin against him and him alone more than we can ever know. His anger against our sin is greater than we dare to admit. We know not how or when or where to come to him. Here is the miracle. He grabbed hold of us before the world began. He saved us, for "while we were still sinners, Christ died for us." Again and again he makes the first move, coming to us.

In our reading the miracle unfolds. Jesus comes in more than promise; he comes himself. He comes not as judge and destroyer, as well he could, but he comes in the flesh as one of us.

"Tired as he was from the journey," our text reads. How encouraging those words are. He knows and understands, for he "was tempted in every way, just as we are—yet was without sin." He gives us what we could never give ourselves. He gives us freedom from death, because he entered death and broke its power. He gives us peace, because he brings us back together with God. He offers us help for our every need. And he is there when we need him.

It was no accident that Jesus sat by this well, alone. He was waiting for someone to come; someone who needed him desperately. And he would be there. He is always there. He has come to each of us in our baptism and taken us for himself. He enters and stays in our lives. He remains always close to us. For he is not far from any one of us. We have his Word. We have him as we receive his very body and blood in the sacrament. By these means, he embraces us and remains with us always.

Dear Lord Jesus, left to ourselves, we would never find you. We thank you that you have found us and that you have forgiven our sins. We rejoice that you take us as we are and that you make us over again. We know that you remain with us in Word and sacrament. Continue to be with us and ever hold us fast until we are with you forever. Amen.

When Jesus landed and saw a large crowd, he had compassion on them and healed their sick. (Matthew 14:14)

MEETING OUR REAL NEEDS

Compassion leads to action. Jesus not only felt, he acted.

Matthew gives us a summary statement here: "and Jesus healed them." The other three gospel writers fill in the details. Mark writes, "So he began teaching them many things." Luke comments, "He welcomed them and spoke to them about the kingdom of God, and healed those who needed healing."

Jesus, as true God, saw the real needs of these people—both spiritual and physical. He saw how desperate and forlorn they were, like sheep without a shepherd. As the great Physician, he would treat not only the symptoms, but also the cause. The physical ailments and needs these people had were only the symptoms of a much greater disease: the sickness of sin. If Jesus were to address only the physical, it would have been like treating a brain tumor with aspirin.

Jesus' first priority was their spiritual depravity. He instructed them from the Word of God about the kingdom of God. This kingdom, which God had promised to David and his descendants, was to be established by David's Son, Jesus of Nazareth, who stood before them. This would not be a physical or worldly kingdom, but a spiritual kingdom—established within them through faith in him, the Christ of God.

Having cared for their souls, our healing Lord now attended to their bodies. Those who had physical ills he healed immediately and completely. His power to heal physical ills reinforced the truth of his power to heal their spiritual ills.

The compassion of our Lord is not restricted to our spiritual ills. He is also concerned with our physical health. He has created our bodies with tremendous recuperative powers. He has given physicians and surgeons the skills and technology needed to treat severe physical ills. He wants us to appreciate and use them as gifts and blessings from him.

We have a healing Lord. Let us not forget this. Go to him for healing—spiritual and physical.

Be thou our Joy and Brightness,
Our Cheer in pain and loss,
Our Sun in darkest terror,
The Glory round our cross,
A Star for sinking spirits,
A Beacon in distress,
Physician, Friend, in sickness,
In death our Happiness.

O Lord, our great Physician, you know our needs, both physical and spiritual. Send us your healing power. Amen.

Jesus said again, "I tell you the truth, I am the gate for the sheep." (John 10:7)

OUR GOOD SHEPHERD OFFERS PROTECTION

If a shepherd could use only one word in describing the sheep under his care, the word he would probably choose is "helpless." Why "helpless"? Because sheep truly are helpless animals. They cannot defend themselves from predators. They easily lose their way and become lost. Sometimes they cannot even find food that is as close as thirty feet away!

A good shepherd knows this. To care for them he knows he must provide constant, abiding protection.

Our Lord Jesus knows that we also need constant, abiding protection. This is one of the reasons he calls himself "the gate" in today's reading. Shepherds in Bible times often would spend the night in the gateway of the sheep pen. By doing this, predators could not get in nor could sheep wander away without their shepherds knowing it.

The moment the Holy Spirit creates faith in our heart we come under the ever-watchful eye of our Good Shepherd. While a human shepherd may doze and sleep, God's Word assures us, "He who watches over you will not slumber; indeed, he who watches over Israel will neither slumber nor sleep. . . . The Lord will keep you from all harm—he will watch over your life; the Lord will watch over your coming and going both now and forevermore."

Death and destruction, heartache and hurt are all around us. They are caused by sin. And like predators they threaten to overwhelm us. If we were on our own, we would surely fall. But our Shepherd is there. He stands between us and our enemies and promises, "Fear not, for I have redeemed you; I have called you by name; you are mine. When you pass through the waters I will be with you; and when you pass through the rivers, they will not sweep over you."

Our sinful hearts may tempt us to wander along dangerous ways. But once again, our Shepherd is there to protect us. Like a gate he stands in our way and turns us back to safety.

He is by our side constantly, around the clock. He is ready to help in every time of need. How blessed are we!

Yea, tho' I walk in death's dark vale,
Yet will I fear no ill;
For Thou art with me, and Thy rod
And staff me comfort still. Amen.

The thief comes only to steal and kill and destroy; I have come that they may have life and have it to the full. (John 10:10)

HE IS THE LIFESAVER OF HIS FLOCK

Sometimes the shepherd's life is a dangerous one. David tells us of two such instances in 1 Samuel 17:34,35: "When a lion or a bear came and carried off a sheep from the flock, I went after it, struck it and rescued the sheep from its mouth. When it turned on me, I seized it by its hair, struck it and killed it. Your servant has killed both the lion and the bear."

David risked his own life for the sake of his sheep. He did it willingly. He did it out of love. He did it because he was a good shepherd.

The Bible tells us that Jesus not only risked his life, he gave his life as "the atoning sacrifice for our sins, and not only for ours but also for the sins of the whole world." Jesus is the Good Shepherd. He saw us hopelessly caught in the grasp of sin and trapped in the jaws of death. We could not escape. Because he is both true God and true man, only Jesus Christ could help us; and he did not hesitate to come to our rescue.

Christ did not fail. He saved his sheep by laying down his life for them. God's law had demanded death as punishment for sin, and Jesus took upon himself the punishment we deserved. He died in our place. We surely did not merit such sacrifice and love. As the hymnwriter says:

> *What punishment so strange*
> *is suffered yonder!*
> *The Shepherd dies for sheep*
> *that loved to wander.*

What love our Good Shepherd has for us! What pain he suffered for us! He truly is our Savior, our lifesaver! Because of his resurrection we know we have life in his name. And in addition to such a gracious gift, our Lord promises us much more! "He who did not spare his own Son, but gave him up for us all—how will he not also, along with him, graciously give us all things?" How can we ever thank God for giving us such a Good Shepherd? May we daily ask the Holy Spirit to fill us with love and gratitude, that our whole life will be one hearty "thank you" to our Good Shepherd, our lifesaver.

Perverse and foolish, oft I strayed,
But yet in love He sought me
And on His shoulder gently laid
And home, rejoicing, brought me. Amen.

And there shall be one fold and one Shepherd. (John 10:16)

THE RULING SHEPHERD

Jesus concludes the picture of himself as the Good Shepherd by describing his flock. Jesus' sheep are his believers. He gathers them from every age and nation by the power of his gospel. They are young and old, male and female, Jew and Gentile, rich and poor. Yet together they constitute one flock under the one Shepherd.

Jesus is speaking here of his church. The church is one, not in the sense of being one outward, visible organization, but one in the blessed fellowship of faith which binds together all who follow Jesus as their Good Shepherd. Its members are all who, by the Spirit's work in their hearts, believe that Jesus took their sins away through his death on the cross. They listen to his voice and follow him. Through the gospel they know him and look forward to eternal life with him. This spiritual flock makes no racial or social distinctions. It breaks down every barrier and brings all who believe in Jesus as their Savior together into his one fold.

The Good Shepherd leads and rules his flock. He knows his sheep, and he guides them. He speaks to them in his Word, providing them with all they need to remain in the fold. He governs the events of history to serve the welfare of his flock. And on the last day he will make his one fold, now invisible, visible in heaven.

Like every other aspect of Jesus' picture of himself as the Good Shepherd, his assurance that he is the One Shepherd ruling over his one flock is rich in comfort. Though to the world we appear to be in the most miserable, scattered and unattended condition, in reality the very opposite is true. For we are all members of the undivided Body of Christ. We all have been baptized with one and the same baptism. We worship one Lord, who is above all and through all and who dwells by faith in the hearts of all who worship him. Though plagued and tempted and persecuted, we look for strength to the same heavenly Father and follow the voice of the same Good Shepherd. And in heaven we shall rejoice together forever in the sunshine of his love.

Few pictures in Scripture are as rich in comfort, joy and peace as is the picture of Jesus as our Good Shepherd. May he bless us with his Word and preserve us as his sheep, here and in eternity!

Come, faithful Shepherd, feed Thy sheep;
In Thine own arms the lambs enfold.
Give help to climb the heavenward steep
Till Thy full glory we behold. Amen.

"I am the good shepherd. The good shepherd lays down his life for the sheep. . . . No one takes it from me, but I lay it down of my own accord. I have authority to lay it down and authority to take it up again." (John 10:11,18)

THE GOOD SHEPHERD LAYS DOWN HIS LIFE

Was he a victim of circumstances? In no way. On the contrary, he was the author of the circumstances! He was in control, doing exactly what had to be done. To lay down his life was the purpose for which he had come. No one could keep him from it. Long ago this had been planned and authorized by his heavenly Father.

The good shepherd's plan to lay down his life for his sheep is the central theme of the Bible. The death of the Messiah was announced after the fall into sin. It was repeatedly announced throughout the time of the Old Testament. It is the focus of the New Testament.

But in all of Scripture there is no passage that portrays this theme more clearly than Isaiah's prophecy in chapter 53. "Surely he took up our infirmities and carried our sorrows, yet we considered him stricken by God, smitten by him, and afflicted. But he was pierced for our transgressions, he was crushed for our iniquities; the punishment that brought us peace was upon him, and by his wounds we are healed. We all, like sheep, have gone astray, each of us has turned to his own way; and the LORD has laid on him the iniquity of us all." Here we see, with a clarity unsurpassed in the Bible, a picture of the good shepherd laying down his life for the sheep.

It is your shepherd who speaks these words. He speaks them to you to comfort you with the forgiveness of sins. It cost his life, but he considered your salvation worth the cost.

Why did he do it? To gather a people who would live for him and serve him. The Apostle Peter (himself a wayward sheep at times) summed it up like this: "He himself bore our sins in his body on the tree, so that we might die to sins and live for righteousness; by his wounds you have been healed. For you were like sheep going astray, but now you have returned to the Shepherd and Overseer of your souls."

Dear Savior and Good Shepherd, what tremendous love I see in your death on the cross. It was for wayward sheep like me that you died. The punishment that you suffered brought me peace with God. Help me to see that message as the focal point of your Word. To thank you, I will serve you with my entire life. Amen.

"I have other sheep that are not of this sheep pen. I must bring them also. They too will listen to my voice, and there shall be one flock and one shepherd." (John 10:16)

CHRIST, THE GOOD SHEPHERD FOR ALL

Of all the titles which Jesus claims for himself, no doubt "The Good Shepherd" is one of the most revealing and comforting to the Christian. A real shepherd will always be concerned about his sheep. He will not only look after the entire flock, leading it to green pasture and good water and protecting it from vicious animals that would destroy the sheep, but as a good shepherd will be interested and concerned about the well-being of each individual sheep in his flock. He calls each one by name, gives it special care and attention when it is sick or injured, searches for it when it has strayed from the flock.

A sheep is among the most helpless of all creatures when left to itself. When straying, it will wander away until it is completely lost, for it does not have a sense of direction to guide it home. It is unable to find good pasture by itself. It cannot scent and find good water to drink. It is not equipped to defend itself from it's natural enemies. Left to itself, it would soon perish of hunger and thirst in a wilderness or fall an easy victim to vicious animals. But this is also a picture of man as he is by nature. The prophet Isaiah describes man's condition by saying: "All we like sheep have gone astray; we have turned everyone to his own way."

But Jesus, the Good Shepherd, has come "to seek and to save that which was lost." He was sent by the Father "unto the lost sheep of the house of Israel." He was born of the Jews, lived and worked and carried out his public ministry and completed God's plan of salvation in Israel. But that did not mean that salvation was intended only for them. In our text Jesus says: "Other sheep I have, which are not of this fold; them also I must bring." The Good Shepherd has in mind the multitudes of Gentiles who are lost without a shepherd's care. Them also he has come to seek and to save. God "will have all men to be saved, and to come unto the knowledge of the truth." Jesus is the Good Shepherd for all.

It matters not who we are, where we live, what we have done; Jesus had us in mind, too. Though we may have been wandering far from our Good Shepherd, lost and in danger of perishing eternally, Jesus has come to seek us and to bring us safely into his fold.

Lord, help us to heed the voice of our Good Shepherd so that we may follow him in faith as he leads us into his eternal fold. Amen.

"Peace I leave with you; my peace I give you. I do not give to you as the world gives. Do not let your hearts be troubled and do not be afraid. You heard me say, 'I am going away and I am coming back to you.' If you loved me, you would be glad that I am going to the Father, for the Father is greater than I. I have told you now before it happens, so that when it does happen you will believe." (John 14:27-29)

JESUS GIVES US HIS PEACE

Martin Luther found a great deal of comfort in these words of Holy Scripture. Luther knew that he had not deserved eternal life from a holy God. Therefore when the Savior announced, "Peace I leave with you," these words filled his heart with joy.

Many people today, unfortunately, do not share Luther's attitude toward sin. As far as the world is concerned, sin is only a "sickness" or a "weakness" in the human soul. Because the world does not view sin as a real problem, the world does not appreciate the Savior's announcement of real peace. Unless we first of all learn to confess, "Lord, I am by nature sinful and unclean; I also have sinned against you in thought, word and deed," the Savior's words will mean nothing to us.

But after God's law has shown us how poor and wretched and needy we really are, then the Savior's words of comfort bring great joy to our hearts. "Peace I leave with you; my peace I give you. . . . Do not let your hearts be troubled and do not be afraid." His peace is not another kind of temporary peace such as the world has to offer. It is a peace between God and us. It is a permanent peace, the peace of knowing that God will give us every blessing, for Jesus' sake. It is the peace which settled over the disciples once they realized that Jesus had risen from the grave. It is the peace which the Holy Spirit, the Comforter, brought to them and still brings to us through the gospel.

This peace, which is ours in Christ, is the cause for endless joy. Jesus has now returned to the throne of his Father's majesty on high. Jesus did humble himself—even to the extent of dying a shameful death on the cross. And he did it all for us. But now Jesus, having completed his work here on earth, sits in glory at the right hand of the Father. From his exalted position in heaven Jesus continues to assure us, "My peace I give you!" And he offers it to us again and again through his Word and Sacraments.

The peace of this world may be very attractive, but it is also very temporary. The peace which Jesus offers, on the other hand, though it appears much less attractive, even irrelevant, to the eyes of men, is real and eternal.

Grant us your peace, O Lord! Amen.

On the evening of the first day of the week, when the disciples were together, with the doors locked for fear of the Jews, Jesus came and stood among them and said, "Peace be with you!" (John 20:19)

THE GIFT OF PEACE

The disciples had deserted Jesus, denied him and ignored his promises. In his suffering and death Jesus had been left to stand alone. But now he was standing among them. He had not forsaken his disciples as they had forsaken him. In fact, he did not even come to them with harsh words of rebuke and scorn. He came to them with peace.

The Lord has not left us alone either. He has promised to be with us always, even to the end of the world. And on Pentecost, Christ sent his Holy Spirit to comfort and direct his church on earth, until that day when we can stand with our Lord in the rooms of his Father's heavenly home.

In this world people have attempted to find peace through treaties, wars to end wars, nuclear arms, drugs and the like. But sin, hatred, anger, bloodshed, violence and wars continue to fill the headlines of life. And yet, no matter how much trouble we see in this life, we Christians still possess the gift of peace, which Jesus gave to his disciples that evening.

We cannot explain this peace to an unbeliever, because it surpasses all human understanding. But we know what it means for us. It is peace with our conscience, when we know that our sins are forgiven in Christ. It is peace with God, when we look to the cross of Christ as full payment for all our sins. It is peace of mind, when we cast all our cares upon the Lord, who cares for us. It is the hope of eternal peace, as we look forward to the coming of our Lord on Judgment Day. It is a peaceful night's rest, as we leave behind the tensions of the day in prayer.

We don't deserve this gift of peace any more than the disciples did in that locked room. And we certainly cannot make this peace for ourselves. It is another daily evidence of the miraculous grace of God, with which he continues to love us, in spite of our own sin and unfaithfulness. There is nothing else in the world like it. As Jesus assures us, "Peace I leave with you; my peace I give you. I do not give to you as the world gives. Do not let your hearts be troubled and do not be afraid."

O Lord, we give you thanks for the gift of peace, which you have so graciously bestowed upon us. May the power and comfort of your Spirit calm our troubled hearts, until the day of your coming. Amen.

Jesus . . . said, "Peace be with you!" After he said this, he showed them his hands and side. (John 20:19,20)

THE PRICE OF PEACE

Almost thirty million fatalities and more than one trillion dollars! That, history tells us, was the staggering cost of World War II. Of course, such bare statistics do not tell the whole story. Only those who lived through the war can do that. Only they can tell of loved ones who went away to war never to be seen again, of people displaced from their homes and never allowed to return, of the terrible economic sacrifice and the lingering emotional and psychological trauma suffered by so many of the war's victims.

As great as the cost of World War II was, what if the outcome of the war had been different and our freedom had been lost? Then the cost would have been even greater! We may be sad that all that money and all those lives were spent, but we rejoice that they were not spent in vain. We rejoice that the cost of the war became the price of peace. Peace did come. It was peace with honor and freedom.

In the same way we find both tragedy and joy in the sufferings, death and crucifixion of our Savior. It was tragic that the very Son of God had to die because of the sins of men. It was tragic that the most precious blood in the world had to be shed. It was tragic that the most loving Father there ever was had to turn his back on the most loving and perfect Son there ever was, if only for a short time. In fact, we can think of no greater tragedy in all the world than this.

Yet this was the price of our peace, peace with God, a glorious peace, a lasting peace, a peace that gives us joy and freedom as God's dear children. Our hearts are filled with sadness when we see what a great price was paid for our peace, but at the same time we are most happy and grateful that that price was paid. Our Lord's pierced hands and wounded side bring tears to our eyes, but they are also reason for joy. They tell us that our sins are gone.

How, then, can any of us continue to live in sin as if nothing has happened? As those who suffered through World War II surely said, "Never again!" and increased their vigilance against tyranny, so we who have escaped an even greater, eternal disaster ought to cleanse our hearts and lives to act like the children of God he wants us to be. We have ample reason to shun sin and all its shame. All we need to do is to consider his love and the price of our peace.

Thank you, Lord, for paying the great price that was necessary for our peace. Amen.

Jesus came and stood among them and said, "Peace be with you!" After he said this, he showed them his hands and side. The disciples were overjoyed when they saw the Lord. (John 20:19,20)

NO ORDINARY PEACE

On the evening of that first Easter day the disciples were full of fears, disappointments and doubts. Their Lord Jesus was dead. Now that he had allowed himself to be crucified, how could he be the earthly king some of them were looking for? And how could he be their Savior from sin? A dead Savior cannot save.

Furthermore, it might only be a matter of time before the authorities came knocking on the door and took them away. And even if the reports of the women, of Simon and of the two from Emmaus were true, even if Jesus were alive, why would he want anything to do with them? Hadn't they all forsaken him and fled? They had betrayed him. They had given up their faith. Surely, they would never see him again.

No wonder the disciples were overjoyed when Jesus suddenly appeared among them. Not only was he alive, not only had the enemy not defeated him, but Jesus was not at all angry with them. In one short statement he immediately assured them that he had forgiven them everything. "Peace be with you!" he said.

Who can measure what those words mean to us today? There are times when we, like the disciples, are in the depths of despair. It may be that a loved one has left us, some fond hope has been dashed to pieces, or sin has taken such a toll that we wonder whether the Lord will ever have anything to do with us again. But then Jesus says to us, "Peace be with you!" And immediately the darkness and gloom disappear. We are forgiven. We are still God's and he is still ours. He is at peace with us.

This is no ordinary peace, but the peace of knowing that our eternal future is secure. This is no temporary armistice between warring nations or quarreling neighbors, this is an eternal peace with God established for all people for all time.

Stories are told of news reporters near the end of World War II hoping to be the first to tell the world that peace had finally arrived. Oh, the happy person who would be the first to break the news! But if the news of that armistice was worthy to be passed on, so is the news of the peace we have with God through the shedding of Jesus' blood. Surely that, more than any other, is no ordinary peace, and the news of it should be spread to the four corners of the earth.

Lord, lead us to treasure your peace more than any other. Amen.

The disciples were overjoyed when they saw the Lord. (John 20:20)

HAPPINESS IS . . .

"**H**appiness is a warm slice of banana bread right out of the oven, smothered with butter." Or "happiness is a warm puppy." We make such statements, but do we really believe that's what happiness is? Banana bread soon gets cold and stale. Puppies soon grow up. God's creation is so wonderful that we find a little bit of happiness in a lot of things, but lasting happiness is hard to find.

For most people happiness is something that's just around the corner. They almost have it, but not yet. Ask a child, and he may tell you that happiness is finally being old enough to go to school. Ask the person who's in school, and he may tell you that happiness is getting out of school, getting his first job, and being on his own. Ask the family man, and he may tell you that happiness will come when the children are grown, when he's retired and finally has the time to do all the things he's always wanted to do. Ask the retired person, and he may tell you that he hasn't quite found happiness either. Like a mirage in the desert, happiness seems to move away just when we get close.

What was it that made the disciples happy that first Easter evening? They saw Jesus! "The disciples were overjoyed when they saw the Lord." Jesus, their Savior, was alive! He had risen from the dead! And he was the same loving friend to them he had always been!

Someday we too will see Jesus, face to face, his arms outstretched, welcoming us home to heaven. Never again will we hunger. Never again will we thirst. There will be no more death or crying or pain, for the old order of things will have passed away. No more will happiness move away just when we get close, but it will cover us like a blanket on the outside, and permeate our whole inner being.

But if happiness is seeing Jesus, let's remember that we don't have to wait until eternity to see him. We can see him today in his Word. In his Word we can already see Jesus loving us, helping us along life's road, forgiving all our sins, interceding for us before our heavenly Father's throne. We can see Jesus being the same friend to us that he was to the disciples. Seeing Jesus in this way not only makes us happy. Like the disciples, we are overjoyed.

Lord, how anxiously we await the joys you have in store for us in heaven. But how happy you have made us already, now that we have seen you in your Word. Amen.

Again Jesus said, "Peace be with you!" (John 20:21)

A WORD OF PEACE—A WORD OF POWER

Have you noticed that whenever a person blesses or curses something by his own authority, nothing really happens? Many a neighbor's dog or errant hammer has been cursed with no apparent result. No lightning came down from heaven to punish the person or thing that was cursed. The accursed thing did not wither away or suddenly disappear. Man's curse is only an empty wish on his part. He huffs and puffs, but accomplishes nothing. And so it is when man blesses by his own authority. He wishes and hopes, but he has no power to make it come to pass. Many a "Bless you!" has been spoken with little result.

But when God blesses or curses, things happen. When God utters a curse, the ground opens up and swallows hundreds of people at once, fire and brimstone come down from heaven and destroy whole cities, and entire armies lose their will to fight. Likewise, when God speaks a blessing. When Jesus told the paralytic that his sins were forgiven and that he should get up and walk, the forgiveness and the healing were contained in his words. It was already done.

God's word is a word of power. When God speaks, things happen. In creation God said, "Let there be!" and there it was. He spoke, and it was done. When God announced that Adam and Eve were banished from the Garden, it was accomplished immediately, perhaps even in mid-sentence and before our first parents could hear all that God said.

So it was also when Jesus stood before his disciples that first Easter evening and said, "Peace be with you!" This was no mere empty wish of a common mortal hoping that his friends would have a nice day. This was a word of power which contained within itself the ability to effect what it expressed. He said, "Peace be with you!" and it was so. The words not only gave comfort, they produced saving faith. They established peace as the disciples believed them.

As the Prince of Peace, Jesus brought about the peace that now exists between God and man. And now he offers that peace to us. He says to each of us, "Peace be with you!" May those words of Jesus be to us, as they were to the disciples, words of power which awaken and strengthen faith. Remember, these are not the words of mortal man. They are words of power which grant the peace of which they speak. Peace is ours. The life, the death and the words of Jesus make it so.

Lord, bless your word of peace that it may be a word of power establishing in our hearts that precious peace which we so earnestly desire. Amen.

After he said this, he showed them his hands and side. The disciples were overjoyed when they saw the Lord. (John 20:20)

THE GIFT OF JOY

I ask you, "How could anyone be overjoyed while looking at someone who has been mortally wounded?" Jesus had been wounded in the hands, feet and side. He was showing these wounds to his disciples, but what was their reaction? Sorrow or sympathy? No. They were overjoyed at seeing their wounded Lord; not because he was wounded, rather because he had risen from the grave.

The wounds of our risen Savior are the marks of victory. They are visible proof that Jesus Christ is true God and true Man, David's Son and David's Lord. When we look upon the wounds of Jesus, we see the wonderful message of our salvation. Eternal God became mortal man, in order to humble himself under his own law. After a life of perfect righteousness, the Lord of all creation gave his life in death, to satisfy the curse of the law upon the sins of all mankind. Because he made full payment for all our sins, the Lord is able to give us forgiveness and salvation.

If we were looking upon the wounds of a dead man lying in a grave, we would have reason to sorrow. But this is Jesus himself showing us his wounds—Jesus, who once was dead but now lives. We have reason to be overjoyed. Every victory celebration is meant to be a joyous occasion. And the gift of joy, which the Lord gave to his disciples, lives on for all eternity. The message of Christ's death and resurrection brought joy to thousands of repentant hearts on the first Pentecost. And it continues to bring joy to countless thousands of sinners all over the world, who have come to know Jesus as their Savior.

The gift of joy in Christ is a wonderful blessing from the Lord. In our daily lives, when frustrations and afflictions bring frowns to our faces, there can still be joy in our hearts. For our Lord is faithful and powerful and promises to deliver us from all evil. And when we Christians face death (be it our own, or that of a loved one), in the midst of sorrow we can know the joy of a personal victory in Christ. For as the Lord rose and lives again, so also in death we live and will rise again.

Only with such joy in his heart could the Apostle Paul have written, "Yes, and I will continue to rejoice. . . . For to me, to live is Christ and to die is gain."

O Lord, fill our hearts with joy in Christ, now and forevermore. Amen.

After he said this, he showed them his hands and side. The disciples were overjoyed when they saw the Lord. (John 20:20)

THE SECRET OF LASTING PEACE AND JOY

A casual reading of the New Testament might lead some to assume that events after our Lord's glorious resurrection were rather scrambled. We know that he appeared to Mary, to the other women and to the disciples on the road to Emmaus. Since Jesus had predicted his return from the grave, we might expect his followers to be waiting with calm hope and living joy. Instead, they brooded in grief. His return from the grave was utterly unexpected.

Luke, chapter 24, informs us that the disciples even doubted the testimony of their own eyes when Jesus appeared to them on Easter Sunday evening. Initially, they thought that he was a ghost. Their fears and doubts must have been frustrating for Jesus.

But Jesus was patient with them. He gently invited them to look at the puncture marks in his hands and feet. He encouraged them to touch him. Even though in his glorified state he no longer needed food, Jesus ate before their eyes, providing their senses ample opportunity to verify that it really was he. Jesus really had risen. He was not a ghost.

What a change came over the disciples' hearts that Easter night! His words and wounds drove despair from their minds and hearts. We can well imagine that they were surprised to see him. Their hearts must have skipped a beat when he suddenly appeared. They forgot their fear of the Jews. Their apprehension vanished. They were certain that Jesus was alive. Hope was revived; confidence was restored. "The disciples were overjoyed when they saw the Lord."

Their joy in the presence of our risen Lord teaches us that the secret of lasting peace and joy lies in looking to the living Lord Jesus. True peace cannot be bought or manufactured. Lasting joy cannot be achieved through money, learning or feverish activity. They are a gift from Jesus. "Therefore, there is now no condemnation for those who are in Christ Jesus" (Romans 8:1). Our God has stopped at nothing to remove the threat of sin, death and hell. Will he not assist us with our lesser fears and anxieties! Let us not shame our Savior by living as if he were still dead!

I am content! Lord, draw me unto Thee
And wake me from the dead
That I may rise forevermore to be
With Thee, my living Head. Amen.

Now Thomas (called Didymus), one of the Twelve, was not with the disciples when Jesus came. So the other disciples told him, "We have seen the Lord!" (John 20:24,25)

IN NEED OF PEACE OF MIND

Three men were talking one day about the frailties of people. Said one man, "The trouble with most people is that they eat too much." The second man objected, and said, "It isn't how much you eat, but what you eat that counts." The third man, a doctor, said, "It's neither what you eat nor how much. It's what's eating you that is important." The doctor hit the nail on the head.

The trouble most people have today is that gnawing inside of them. There are so many things to do. There are so many doubts. There are so many problems to be solved. Each of these eats away at a person's peace of mind. They haunt his waking hours and disturb his sleep.

Thomas had the same problem. Thomas was a faithful follower of the Lord. He loved Jesus with all his heart. In fact, Thomas was one of the first to realize that Jesus would have to die. When Jesus went to Bethany to see his friend Lazarus, it was Thomas who said, "Let us also go that we may die with him." And yet Thomas's heart was filled with uncertainty. When Jesus spoke of the many mansions in his Father's house and of how he would go and prepare a way to those mansions, it was Thomas who said, "Lord, we don't know where you are going, so how can we know the way?" Thomas loved his Lord but wasn't sure what his mission was.

What was true of Thomas was also true of the rest of the disciples. But on the day of our text, the doubts, the questions and the uncertainties were gone for them. They said, "We have seen the Lord. We have seen Jesus. He is alive. He lives." The disciples saw in Christ's resurrection the answer to all the problems in their lives. They wanted Thomas to have that same peace of mind.

Is there someone in your family who needs that peace of mind? Take them to Calvary and from Calvary to the empty tomb. Tell them, "We have seen the Lord." We have found in him the answer to all our problems. He has shown us the way to live and to love, to sing and to shout his glory. No problem, no doubt, no situation is too hopeless, for we have seen the Lord.

Dearest Lord Jesus, we have seen you through the eyes of faith. We know that you are alive and will ever live. Come live in each of our lives with your love. Help us to share you with each other and with those around us. In your name we pray. Amen.

"I am coming to you now, but I say these things while I am still in the world, so that they may have the full measure of my joy within them." (John 17:13)

KEEPING HAPPY

"Is everybody HAPPY?" Thus Al Jolson would begin his comedy routine. He asked the question because he felt a responsibility to make and to keep his audience happy.

The departing Lord Jesus also wanted the disciples he was leaving behind to be happy. He knew that this world does not, as a rule, tend to make its inhabitants happy. He also knew that at this time his disciples were anything but happy. They had begun to realize that he would soon be taken from them in death. Jesus therefore prayed to the Father that they might have the full measure of his joy in them.

The words "his joy" tell us that Jesus himself was happy. Yes, even in the face of betrayal by a disciple; in the face of crucifixion by his own people, Jesus was full of joy. It was not the "keep them rolling in the aisles with jokes" kind of happiness. It was the kind of joy that is quietly confident of victory against impossible odds.

The Lord wanted his disciples to have this kind of joy, then and in the difficult days to come. That is why he was going to the cross to die for them. That is why he would rise again and proclaim his victory over sin and death. That was why he prayed for them as he did—so that they might have the full measure of his joy in them.

Jesus' prayer was answered by the Father. Through his word and the Holy Spirit the disciples were able to rejoice later on, even in the face of persecution. They were happy in their ascended Lord.

How about you and me? Jesus was praying for us in his high priestly prayer as well as for those in the upper room. Are we happy? With life in this world being what it is we can't always expect to be as ecstatic as the disciples were on Easter Sunday. But do we have that quiet joy that comes from knowing that he who died for us is alive again? Do we have the happiness of which the Lord said earlier that night, "No one will take away our joy"? This is the joy that comes from the sure hope of eternal life, the joy that will stay with us even through our darkest days. May the full measure of our Savior's joy find a place in our hearts.

Heavenly Father, there are so many things that make us sad. Give us the full measure of the joy that can be ours only through faith in our risen Lord. Amen.

Now a man named Lazarus was sick. He was from Bethany, the village of Mary and her sister Martha. . . . So the sisters sent word to Jesus, "Lord, the one you love is sick." (John 11:1,3)

A FRIEND IN THE DAY OF TROUBLE

With what body of water mentioned in the Scriptures are we modern-day friends of Jesus most familiar? Most will answer, the Sea of Galilee. On the northwest shore of the Sea of Galilee stood the city of Capernaum. Capernaum served as Jesus' headquarters during the early years of his ministry. Four of his twelve disciples —Peter, James, John and Andrew— had made their living from the Sea of Galilee as commercial fishermen prior to their acceptance of Jesus' call. Several more of Jesus' disciples called Capernaum or one of its suburbs "home."

Occasionally the usually calm Sea of Galilee was lashed by fierce storms. Cyclonic winds would suddenly come swooping down from the high hills that ringed this body of water. Within minutes the Sea of Galilee could become extremely dangerous to anyone caught on its waters. We remember a time when Jesus and his disciples were caught in such a storm.

Most of the time our lives are like the Sea of Galilee on a calm day. Our hearts are light. God seems to be smiling upon us. He daily provides us with all that we need to stay alive and healthy. He brings joy to our hearts with his gospel.

Things apparently had been going well for Mary and Martha and Lazarus. We do not hear that they had any financial worries. They seemed to be enjoying good health. Best of all Jesus was their friend.

But suddenly and unexpectedly Lazarus became seriously ill. One can imagine how concerned Mary and Martha became as Lazarus's condition steadily worsened. Jesus had permitted trouble to come into the lives of his Bethany friends.

But has Jesus ever promised those who believe in him trouble-free earthly lives? No, he has not. Sickness, disease and other evils do occur. Since the fall of man into sin evils of every kind are found in this world. These evils may strike not only the unbelievers, but also those who are Jesus' friends. Sin has made this world a vale of tears. And because of the sin that still clings to us who are Jesus' friends, daily woes and heartaches are all that we deserve.

The Lord Jesus in his infinite wisdom may not immediately subdue every trouble that comes into our lives. May he grant us the grace to accept all things with patience and with confidence in his mercy, as did his three friends in Bethany.

Jesus, Savior, pilot me
Over life's tempestuous sea. Amen.

When he heard this, Jesus said, "This sickness will not end in death. No, it is for God's glory so that God's Son may be glorified through it." (John 11:4)

JESUS PROMISES TO HELP HIS FRIENDS

Sorry, we can't help you! In our society it is becoming more and more difficult to get help in an emergency. Years ago when a doctor received a call for help, he felt duty bound to respond immediately. Today this is not always the case. Some doctors have become quite independent. The mechanical answering device replies: "Sorry, Dr. Jones is not in. Will you please leave a message." Sometimes even a call to the hospital doesn't bring the results we want. Our best decision is to rush the seriously ill person or accident victim to the hospital emergency room and hope the physician on duty is available.

Jesus' friends are never put off, or given the run-around, when they call upon him for help. With Jesus we never have to make an appointment in advance or sign our name to some hospital or insurance forms. To be sure, proper procedure in human affairs dictates that we make such appointments and fill out forms. But how comforting to know that when we call upon Jesus for help, we can count on gaining his attention immediately. Later Mary and Martha found that out.

When their message, "Lord, the one you love is sick," reached Jesus, Jesus at once considered and diagnosed the case, "This sickness will not end in death. No, it is for God's glory so that God's Son may be glorified through it." And we can assume that Jesus asked the messenger who informed him of Lazarus's illness to deliver the response to Mary and Martha.

That response constituted a promise on the part of Jesus, a promise that all would be well with Lazarus—also a promise that God would be glorified. What comforting promises we, too, have, when we turn to Jesus for help: "Call upon me in the day of trouble; I will deliver you, and you will honor me."

The Lord Jesus assures us that he is both willing and able to resolve all of our problems. True, his response to our call for help may not always be what we would like it to be. But Scripture assures us that "all things work together for good to them that love God"!

What God ordains is always good.
He never will deceive me;
He leads me in His own right way,
And never will He leave me. Amen.

When he heard this, Jesus said, "This sickness will not end in death. No, it is for God's glory so that God's Son may be glorified through it." Yet when he heard that Lazarus was sick, he stayed where he was two more days. . . . After he had said this, he went on to tell them, "Our friend Lazarus has fallen asleep; but I am going there to wake him up." . . . So then he told them plainly, "Lazarus is dead." (John 11:4,6,11,14)

JESUS KNOWS WHEN TO HELP HIS FRIENDS

We friends of Jesus may sometimes wish that we were omniscient. Jesus is omniscient, that is, he knows all things. We may wish that we were omniscient so that we could be of greater service to our fellow human beings. Every now and then we learn that someone whom we know and care about is in trouble. We may feel that if only we had known sooner, we might have been able to do something to help.

Jesus, our all-loving Savior, knew exactly when to respond to the illness of this friend, Lazarus, who lived in Bethany. It may surprise us to learn that Jesus deliberately delayed journeying to Bethany for two days. Though Lazarus was seriously ill, Jesus made no immediate move to help. Mary and Martha may have wondered why it took so long for Jesus to arrive. Had he perhaps decided not to come?

But Jesus knew what he was doing. He waited until he could say to his disciples, "Our friend Lazarus is asleep." Lazarus had died. Now it was time to go to Bethany. The disciples, with perhaps the exception of John, did not understand what Jesus meant. "Then said Jesus unto them plainly, 'Lazarus is dead.' "

Why did Jesus wait until Lazarus was dead? Jesus had already answered that question. He had said, "This sickness will not end in death. No, it is for God's glory so that God's Son may be glorified through it." How would Jesus be glorified by a man's death? Or by waiting until Lazarus's body had lain in the tomb for four days? Yes, Jesus waited—he waited until many relatives and friends of the family had arrived in Bethany to offer their condolences to Mary and Martha. But then, when he arrived, Jesus called Lazarus back to life.

As believers, that is, friends of Jesus, we have the comfort that he knows when to help us. He knows that much better than we do. If he was willing to suffer the shame and disgrace of the cross for us, will he not also deliver us in every other need and trouble!

Lord Jesus, grant that we might always be willing to await your answer to our prayers. Amen.

When he heard this, Jesus said, "This sickness will not end in death. No, it is for God's glory so that God's Son may be glorified through it." . . . After he had said this, he went on to tell them, "Our friend Lazarus has fallen asleep; but I am going there to wake him up." (John 11:4,11)

JESUS KNOWS HOW TO HELP HIS FRIENDS

When a loved one suddenly becomes seriously ill, we may be at a loss what to do. Even the doctor may be stymied. If the doctor is unable to diagnose the illness, how can he know what to do? But the Lord Jesus is never at a loss. He always knows how to help. He certainly knew how to help in the case of his friends at Bethany.

How? First of all, by not immediately hastening to Bethany when the message arrived that Lazarus was ill. We are told that Jesus deliberately waited to start out for Bethany until after Lazarus's death. Jesus had no intention of healing Lazarus of his illness. Why not? Because Jesus had something better in mind.

After Lazarus had died, Jesus said to his disciples: "Our friend Lazarus has fallen asleep; but I am going there to wake him up." Jesus here announced that he would be raising Lazarus from death. The disciples did not question what Jesus said. Had they not with their own eyes seen Jesus raise the young man of Nain and the daughter of Jairus from the dead?

But Jesus here was not thinking only of the effect that his raising of Lazarus would have on his disciples. He also was thinking of the salutary effect it was to have upon Mary and Martha and also upon their many relatives and friends—yes, of the effect it would have on all of Jerusalem and Judea.

So Jesus made it a point not to arrive at Bethany until after Lazarus's body had been in the tomb for four days. This meant that the process of decay was already well under way. Recall that Jesus had raised the young man of Nain and the daughter of Jairus shortly after they had died. Unbelieving Jews may have suggested that in those cases the dead person had not really been dead, but only unconscious. In Lazarus's case there was plenty of proof that he was dead. Thus, as Jesus had said, the raising of Lazarus would glorify God.

It did. We are told that the raising of Lazarus made such an impression on people that many came to faith in Jesus (John 11:45).

Lord Jesus, you always know much better than we do how to help us in the troubles that come upon us. Deliver us from every evil. Amen.

On his arrival, Jesus found that Lazarus had already been in the tomb for four days. . . . When Martha heard that Jesus was coming, she went out to meet him, but Mary stayed at home. "Lord," Martha said to Jesus, "if you had been here, my brother would not have died. But I know that even now God will give you whatever you ask." (John 11:17-22)

A FRIEND TO RELY ON

It is said of sports that timing is everything. A mistake in timing can turn a touchdown into a loss of yardage, a home run into a pop-up.

Suspense in the theater is all a matter of timing. "Will the hero arrive in time to save the lady in distress?" Timing can affect our real lives quite dramatically, too. Much of what the world calls success depends on being "in the right place at the right time."

Martha considered timing to be critical in the case of her brother's death. If Jesus had been there, she lamented, Lazarus would not have died. It wasn't that Jesus carried some wonder drug with him to cure diseases. Martha had seen Jesus regularly heal the sick by his divine power, by speaking the word. She knew (such was her faith) that Jesus would have healed Lazarus if he had arrived sooner.

But now it was too late. The touchdown pass was blocked. The ball game was over. Lazarus had died. Or was it too late? Martha undoubtedly remembered the message Jesus sent back when he heard of Lazarus's illness. "This sickness will not end in death," he had said. Jesus had never lied about anything or deceived anyone. Could that mean that he would still work a miracle? Would he raise Lazarus from the dead? He had raised the dead before this on two occasions. The body of Lazarus, however, lay decaying in the grave.

Martha was torn between grief and hope, but her faith told her to rely on Jesus. She could not understand it, but she confessed, "I know that even now God will give you whatever you ask." "Even now!" she said. Her brother lay dead; still she trusted in the Lord.

Jesus always stands ready to help those who believe. He does not abandon us. Let us not abandon him. He gave himself into death to redeem us from sin and death. He opened the way to eternal life for us by rising victorious from the dead. No matter how hopeless we might consider matters to be at times, we still have reason to rely on Christ. By his works and his words, we know he will answer our prayers and give us all that we need.

Blessed Lord Jesus, teach us to trust in you for all things. Amen.

But some of them said, "Could not he who opened the eyes of the blind man have kept this man from dying?" (John 11:37)

A FRIEND WITH OUR BEST INTERESTS AT HEART

Why did this tragedy happen? Why to him? Why to her? Why to them? Why to me? Why now? Why?

How often this question troubles us—"Why?" When the ways of life do not fall into the pattern which we have in our minds, the question, "Why?" rises to the surface. It was no different for the people who knew Jesus, who knew Lazarus and his sisters, Mary and Martha. They all wondered why it had to happen that Lazarus died.

Mary and Martha reasoned this way: Had not Jesus performed many miracles? He gave sight to the blind; he restored hearing to the deaf; he gave speech to the dumb; he made the paralytic walk again. Jesus could have healed Lazarus from his sickness. He had done so many other miracles. Surely he could have helped his dear friend, Lazarus.

Such a question troubles all of us at one time or another. We also wonder why things could not be different; why they could not be the way we would like them to be.

However, when we give serious thought to the matter of why the Lord does what he does, we must again grow thankful that we do not have to decide matters.

We sometimes ask questions touching very basic teachings of the Bible. Why did God make man the way he did? Why did God permit man to fall into sin? Why did God devise the plan of saving man the way he did? Why did God give us his revelation concerning this plan of salvation? Such questions and many more could come to mind if we permitted our reason to run rampant.

All these questions are simply answered—because it is God's will and way! God has his own purpose; his ways are higher than our ways. He knows what is best for us. He has our best interests, that is, the best interests of his believers, at heart at all times. We might ask the question, "Why?" But let us answer it just as quickly —"It is God's will." Let the whys give place to the certain promises of God that we have in our Savior, Jesus Christ. And let us confidently pray with the hymn-writer:

Tho' dark my path and sad my lot,
Let me be still and murmur not
Or breathe the prayer divinely taught,
"Thy will be done." Amen.

Jesus was sleeping. The disciples went and woke him, saying, "Lord, save us! We're going to drown!" (Matthew 8:24,25)

A FRIEND IN TIME OF DANGER

It had been a very busy day for Jesus and his disciples. The hours had passed in teaching and healing the crowds that had gathered around. At sunset Jesus and his disciples stepped into the boat to cross the lake and find time for meditation and communion with the heavenly Father. Jesus lay down in the stern of the ship and was soon asleep.

The storm that raged that night was one of no ordinary violence. The men in the boat had been accustomed to the lake from childhood, as many of them plied the trade of commercial fishing, and they were accustomed to all its moods and dangers. But here was a storm which struck fear to their hearts, and even these experienced men saw themselves heading for a watery grave. It has been said that there are few situations where a man realizes how helpless he is as when he is engulfed in such a devastating storm at sea.

From the midst of this storm comes a cry in the night, "Lord, save us! We're going to drown!" Suddenly they knew that all their skill, their cunning as sailors was of no avail. There was only one who could save them. In their distress they went to the Lord as master of wind and wave, as guardian of their bodies and souls. Facing death, they knew him to be their only help and salvation. And Jesus answered their prayers.

The account of the storm on the lake is an historical incident in the life of our Lord and his disciples. But as we think about it a little further, it also becomes a parable of man's existence. We are the occupants of that boat, crossing the stormy seas of life.

While people have their health, and they seem to be able to control things, there often seems to be only a lukewarm acceptance of Jesus. But when trouble and sickness comes, when the leprosy of their sins begins to eat into their souls, when a serious or terminal illness strikes and storms seem to buffet them on every side, then they want to know that Christ is there at their side, that he is the One who is able to save. Then sounds forth the cry of distress, "Lord, save us."

And that is the right word, "save." For when we have that, we have all. Jesus came "to seek and to save that which was lost." Jesus does help us in all our undertakings. But the greatest prayer we can bring to Christ is this, "Lord, save me."

Gracious Lord, save us from all dangers, but above all save us for eternity through your precious blood and merit. Amen.

When Jesus had entered Capernaum, a centurion came to him, asking for help. (Matthew 8:5)

JESUS WOULD BE HIS FRIEND

"**D**oris, I have been transferred, again," said her husband. "We have to move to Los Angeles in six weeks."

A soldier of Rome received the same type of orders 2,000 years ago. "Caesar wants you!" The centurion answered his emperor's call to military service and was stationed more than 1,500 miles from Rome in Capernaum of Galilee. It was not the worst place to be on duty in the Roman Empire. Still, it was not home either.

The centurion could sulk—after all he was far removed from loved ones and friends, or he could resolve to make the best of it. There would be new things to see . . . a new culture to learn . . . and new friends to make.

Plus, he had promised to serve the emperor by being the best possible representative of his country. There would be plenty to do to keep busy, soldiering and otherwise.

While in Capernaum, this officer heard of and committed his allegiance to the Lord of lords and King of kings—Jesus Christ. We don't know exactly when or how it happened; that is not important. It is important that it did happen.

Jesus, his Savior, would conquer his sin and remove the fear of death even in a far-off land. Jesus would be his friend—someone this soldier could go to when he was lonely. Now, there would always be available strength and limitless comfort no matter where he would be stationed. Capernaum was a comfortable place to be after all!

A change of address can often be traumatic. Moving because of work, age or serving our country in the armed services can be cause for some worry, even some fears. What will it be like there? Whom will I meet? Who will replace my former friends and neighbors?

On the other hand, some things never change. Even though a move means change, Jesus Christ, our Savior and Friend who is the same yesterday, today and tomorrow, will be waiting for us when we move to our new city and into our new home. It is comforting for every Christian to know this.

Oh, spread Thy covering wings around
Till all our wanderings cease
And at our Father's loved abode
Our souls arrive in peace. Amen.

In that day you will no longer ask me anything. I tell you the truth, my Father will give you whatever you ask in my name. Until now you have not asked for anything in my name. Ask and you will receive, and your joy will be complete. Though I have been speaking figuratively, a time is coming when I will no longer use this kind of language but will tell you plainly about my Father. In that day you will ask in my name. I am not saying that I will ask the Father on your behalf. No, the Father himself loves you because you have loved me and have believed that I came from God. (John 16:23-27)

WHAT A FRIEND WE HAVE IN JESUS

To the Philippians (4:6) Paul wrote, "In everything, by prayer and petition, with thanksgiving, present your requests to God." These words are preceded by the saying, "Do not be anxious about anything." They present the Bible's own remedy for worry, the sure cure for care. That cure for care is prayer in all cases.

People try to cope with their cares in many different ways but somehow always seem to neglect the sure and effective way. Some drag their worries around with themselves all day long. They get up with their problem in the morning and take it to bed with them at night. That is folly, useless folly. Others with sublime and supreme indifference shrug off their problems or assume they can drink or dance them away. That's folly, too.

We are not to hoard our worries, as the miser hoards his money. We are not to toss them blithely into the blue, as the gambler casts a pair of dice. We are not to entrust them primarily and exclusively to our fellow men, who often are unable or unwilling to help us. No matter what the case or the care may be, we are to let our requests be made known to God by prayer and supplication with thanksgiving.

This is the God who sent his Son into the world as the Savior from sin. The love he manifested then still reaches out to gather in our requests. The believer who trusts in God and embraces the merits of his Son will be able to send his supplications and thanksgiving up to the throne of grace. He will be able to pray as a dear child to his dear Father in heaven.

The time will come when prayers are no longer needed, but that will not be before the final judgment. Until then we can drive away all cares and worries by requesting the aid of our all-powerful, all-wise, all-merciful Father in heaven. He will help us and bless us.

Lord, I come to Thee for rest,
Take possession of my breast;
There Thy blood-bought right maintain
And without a rival reign. Amen.

Jesus answered her, "If you knew the gift of God and who it is that asks you for a drink, you would have asked him and he would have given you living water." "Sir," the woman said, "you have nothing to draw with and the well is deep. Where can you get this living water? Are you greater than our father Jacob, who gave us the well and drank from it himself, as did also his sons and his flocks and herds?" (John 4:10-12)

JESUS, FRIEND OF SINNERS

Nothing about his appearance gave any hint. He looked like just another ordinary traveler. Yet he made great promises, offering more than the ancient patriarch himself. She wondered to herself, "What can he give me?"

We remember the beggar who sat on the temple steps. He was lame from the time of his birth. As he saw the apostles Peter and John approaching, he too wondered, "What will they give me?" "Can they give me anything?" What a surprise he received. No silver or gold, but the greatest of gifts—he walked for the first time. He came to faith in the Savior of all men. He was given salvation.

We may have wondered, "What can he give us?" The answer is plain. He gives us God's own righteousness. Because he suffered and died in our place, he gives us the forgiveness of sins. What we do not deserve, what we could not earn, is ours as a gift. He wipes away our sin. He covers us with the robe of his righteousness. He washes away every stain and spot.

Through that forgiveness he makes us members of his family. He teaches us that God is our Father. How important! We finally know who we are. Our search is over; we have found our roots. We have an identity. With his help, we begin to live differently. We aim for those things which are good and pleasing in his sight. We live more for him than for ourselves.

We look to the future with confidence. Our life still remains a mystery to us. There is much that we do not understand. But we know that whatever happens will turn out for the best. Above all we know what the end will be. He has promised to return. He has promised to take us with him to be members of his family forever. He has promised us eternal life. And we know that he gives what he promises.

Dear Jesus, we could never come to life without you. Open our eyes to see the greatness of the treasures you offer us. Continue to forgive us. Enable us to live as members of your family. Help us not to lose our way or to become discouraged. Keep our hearts fixed on the promise of your return and eternal life. Amen.

Soon afterward, Jesus went to a town called Nain, and his disciples and a large crowd went along with him. As he approached the town gate, a dead person was being carried out—the only son of his mother, and she was a widow. And a large crowd from the town was with her. (Luke 7:11,12)

DEATH—WHERE LIFE BEGINS

Nain means "pleasantness" or "beauty." But there was nothing pleasant or beautiful the day Jesus came to a town called Nain. There were only tears and death.

Our Lord had just come from the town of Capernaum, where he healed a centurion's servant. As a result of this miracle, a large crowd followed Jesus as he walked a day's journey southwest of Capernaum to the slopes of Little Hermon, where Nain was located. When Jesus came near the gate of the town, he saw a dead man being carried out. It was a gloomy event, at least for many of the people. Death, humanly speaking, is the loss of everything. But Jesus knew otherwise. There was hope which he alone could bring. He alone could offer and present hope because he alone is the Prince of Hope and the Prince of Life.

As visitors and travelers on this earth, we observe death everywhere. We open the newspaper and read the obituary column; we drive downtown and pass a funeral home; we tour the countryside and see a cemetery. Death is all around us, and the words of St. Paul in Romans 6:23 pierce our ears and hearts: "For the wages of sin is death!" No one looks forward to death. However, if we look at the perfect redeeming work of the Visitor who came to Nain, we see that he has power over sin and death.

Because of Jesus we don't have to fear death any more than our bed. Thankfully, St. Paul's Romans 6:23 passage does not stop at a dead end, but rather tells us, that for all who believe in Christ, that is where life begins—eternal life! Listen closely to Paul's entire passage: "For the wages of sin is death, but the gift of God is eternal life in Christ Jesus our Lord."

He gives us hope and peace and life. With his promises in view, each new sunrise reminds us that a glorious eternal day will dawn for us. And the evening shadows teach us to say with childlike confidence:

Now I lay me down to sleep;
I pray the Lord my soul to keep.
If I should die before I wake,
I pray the Lord my soul to take. Amen.

When the Lord saw her, his heart went out to her and he said, "Don't cry." (Luke 7:13)

DON'T CRY!

On November 11, 1975, the Edmund Fitzgerald, a 721-foot ore ship, was on a run from Superior, Wisconsin, to Whitefish Bay, Ontario. It never reached its destination. The high winds and 30-foot waves of Lake Superior made this journey its last one. Twenty-nine men died. The relatives of these sailors were all too familiar with tragedies of this kind. And pain filled their hearts as they heard the church bell ring 29 times. Other mariners and friends were filled with compassion for the surviving families, but nothing could be done. Only words of sympathy could be offered.

The same feelings of compassion filled the heart of Jesus as he approached the gate of Nain and the widow, the corpse, the mournful procession. He came up to her and said, "Don't cry!" Jesus was not implying that it is wrong to cry at a funeral. We know that Jesus wept at the grave of his friend, Lazarus, and we know the Bible says, "Mourn with those who mourn" (Romans 12:15). Tears have a way of releasing the buildup of our sorrow. The message Jesus wanted to communicate to the widow of Nain was this: "Dry your eyes, for you have hope."

Jesus wants to communicate that same message to us today. He wants us to know that we have hope—eternal hope. The Apostle Paul spelled out that hope to the Thessalonian Christians: "Brothers, we do not want you to be ignorant about those who fall asleep, or to grieve like the rest of men, who have no hope. We believe that Jesus died and rose again and so we believe that God will bring with Jesus those who have fallen asleep in him" (1 Thessalonians 4:13,14).

"Stop crying" sounds like an unbelievable request, especially when we see a loved one lowered into the grave. But the message of the forgiveness of sins and the good news of Jesus' love and mercy enables us in due time to dry our tears. They impart the certain hope that we and all who believe in Christ will meet again, nevermore to die.

For the same Christ who said, "Arise!" to the widow's son and, "Come forth!" to Lazarus, will say the same to his people on the last day. And we shall arise and come forth.

Why do we mourn departing friends
Or shake at death's alarms?
'Tis but the voice that Jesus sends
To call them to his arms. Amen.

Then he went up and touched the coffin, and those carrying it stood still. He said, "Young man, I say to you, get up!" (Luke 7:14)

A SUMMONS FROM THE SAVIOR

Imagine yourself following the pallbearers to the graveside. Suddenly a stranger approaches, stops the procession, raises the lid on the coffin, and commands the corpse to sit up. Would there be a few eyebrows raised? Most likely everyone would wonder if the person was in his right mind. Yet, if we simply read the words of our text, it's quite clear that this is exactly what Jesus did. He walked up to the bier, that is, the bed on which the dead man lay, and said, "Get up!" He did not use any theatrical devices. There was no puff of smoke, no spotlight, no drum roll. Jesus just spoke the word. It was by his own power that Jesus ordered this young dead man to arise. And to the amazement of all, he arose.

We might recall that it was this same power that the disciples were given when they first went out to spread the gospel. It was the word of the Lord which allowed the lame to walk and the deaf to hear. And Psalm 33:6 makes it easy for us to believe that it is so. There the psalmist reminds us, "By the word of the LORD were the heavens made, their starry host by the breath of his mouth." If God could do the greater, namely, create the universe and all that is in it, out of nothing, simply by speaking the word—so he can certainly do the lesser, that is, knit a soul and body, which has already been created, back together again.

God's Word, the Bible, is still effective today. The Holy Spirit comes to us in that Word, convinces us of our complete sinfulness and guilt before God, and convinces us that in Christ God has put away our sin and guilt. And we believe and confess that that same word of God will search out every corner of the globe on judgment day and call forth all the dead. Then the unbelievers will be assigned to eternal punishment and the believers to eternal joy.

Some may raise their eyebrows at this teaching. Others will ridicule it. But when the day arrives, and Christ says, "Get up"—all will get up, like it or not. For God's Word is powerful and true. And all who believe it look forward to the last day and that final summons from our Savior: "Come, you who are blessed by my Father; take your inheritance, the kingdom prepared for you since the creation of the world" (Matthew 25:34).

"Forever with the Lord!"
Amen! so let it be.
Life from the dead is in that word,
'Tis immortality. Amen.

The dead man sat up and began to talk, and Jesus gave him back to his mother. (Luke 7:15)

A DEAD MAN SPEAKS

The motion picture industry can produce amazing happenings. It can put us on a wagon train and transport us across the Great Plains. It can strap us in a fantastic spaceship bound for Mars and bring us safely back. A good camera and a good imagination can produce illusions in endless variety.

But on this otherwise ordinary day in the Galilean village of Nain there were no movie cameras and no special effects—just historical facts. A young man who was dead sat up and spoke. The miracle was clear. Everyone who witnessed it knew it for what it was. Only crass unbelief tries to write it off as a hoax or dismiss it as an illusion.

The Bible is filled with many similar events that are out of the ordinary, but true, like the feeding of the 5,000 with only five barley loaves and two small fish, Jesus' walking on the water and the healing of the blind man. As believers in Christ, we accept these miracles as true. Our confession is that of the Apostle Paul, who said, "We live by faith, not by sight" (2 Corinthians 5:7).

Yet we know that the devil, the world and our sinful flesh try to destroy that faith which the Holy Spirit has put into our hearts through baptism, the Lord's Supper and the message of the Bible. Oh, how we continually need the Holy Spirit's help to flee every temptation! We daily need to pray: "I do believe; help me overcome my unbelief!" (Mark 9:24).

Today's Bible reading is one of the weapons by which we are able to overcome the enemy. It clearly tells us that this dead man from Nain sat up and spoke and that Jesus presented him to his mother. We do not know what the young man said, but we do know that he did speak and that he went back home again with his mother. It was not an illusion. It was a fact. And this fact and all the other Bible facts still remain true today. It is true that the Son of God came to this earth as a baby; he lived a perfect life and died for our sins; he physically rose from the dead, ascended into heaven and will return again. These are facts. And as we read about them, study them and take them to heart, the Holy Spirit convinces us that they are true.

**To thine almighty Spirit be
Immortal glory giv'n,
Whose teachings bring us near to Thee
And train us up for heav'n. Amen.**

They were all filled with awe and praised God. "A great prophet has appeared among us," they said. "God has come to help his people." (Luke 7:16)

GOD IS IN OUR TOWN

The people of Nain said, "God has come to help his people." Their statement was more accurate than some of them may have intended it to be. It was true that God visited his people by bringing a young man back to life. But this miracle was not performed by an ordinary representative of God; this miracle was performed personally by God himself—by the God-man, Jesus Christ. The Apostle Paul once wrote to the Colossian Christians, "For in Christ all the fullness of the Deity lives in bodily form" (Colossians 2:9). The people of Nain had not only seen the miracle in which a dead man came back to life, but they actually saw God himself perform it!

All of this is a mystery to us. The doctrine of the Trinity and of Jesus' incarnation are beyond our comprehension. How can God be in heaven as a spirit (who has no flesh and bones), and at the same time be on earth as a man? We cannot understand this any better now than we did when we were small children. Yet, as when we were children, we believe that it is true.

Although the teaching that God is everywhere is a mystery to our intellect, it is a comfort to our heart. It is comforting to know that wherever we are living, God the Father who made us still continues to preserve us. It is comforting to know that Jesus Christ who redeemed us from sin, still walks next to us in this life. It is comforting to know that God the Holy Spirit who has brought us to faith in Christ, continues to keep us in that faith.

From a spectacular miracle we know that the Triune God was active in the town of Nain about 2,000 years ago. But his Word informs us that he still is active today in our town and among us. It does not matter where we live. For Jesus' sake, our God is with us; he will help us; he will forgive us; he will guide us.

If our doubts ever arise concerning God's presence, all we have to do is turn to Isaiah 41:10 and read God's own words and promises: "Do not fear, for I am with you; do not be dismayed, for I am your God. I will strengthen you and help you; I will uphold you with my righteous right hand." God is with us, that we might reign with him.

**Our God, our Help in ages past,
Our Hope for years to come,
Be Thou our Guard while troubles last
And our eternal Home! Amen.**

When the Lord saw her, his heart went out to her and he said, "Don't cry." Then he went up and touched the coffin, and those carrying it stood still. He said, "Young man, I say to you, get up!" The dead man sat up and began to talk, and Jesus gave him back to his mother. (Luke 7:13-15)

DEATH CANNOT HOLD US

Who is Jesus Christ? "He's our God and our Savior." That's the answer we Christians give, but that isn't the answer the average man on the street gives. "Jesus was a frustrated political reformer." "Jesus was a great teacher who set an excellent example for us to follow in our associations with others." That's what others say.

How can we be sure who's right? Pro-football fans all over the country feel that their team is the best when the season begins, but at the end the contest narrows down to two teams. It's the best of the NFC against the best of the AFC. The winner is undisputed champion because he has beaten the best.

That's what Jesus did. The powers of darkness put their best up against him—death. Mere man would have wilted facing that power. He would have been bombed out of the stadium. But Jesus was no mere man, and when he came face to face with death, death met its conqueror.

The story is a very sad one. A woman who lived at Nain had already lost her husband. Now her son, the last joy and comfort of her life, was dead too. Everyone was very sympathetic. They wanted to help her, but what can anyone do in the face of death? Once a person is dead, all hope is gone. Or is it?

When Jesus and his disciples came along and realized what had happened, we're told that "his heart went out to her." He felt genuinely sorry for her and quickly took an action that turned her sorrow into joy. He stopped the funeral procession, walked up to the dead man, and said, "Young man, get up!"

What a joke it would be for a mere man to try something like that! But Jesus is no mere man. He is our God and our Savior, and even the dead have to obey him. The young man arose! The great enemy, death, could not hold him.

Death could not hold Christ either. It tried! The church and the state of that day crucified Christ. He died. He was buried. But on the third day the grave had to give up its victim again. Death could not hold the Lord Jesus.

Neither will it be able to hold us. The day is coming when all of us will fall asleep in death, but we need not be afraid. There's no reason for us to be afraid, for we have a Savior who met death and conquered it for us!

Jesus, thank you for taking away our fear of death. Amen.

So he replied to the messengers, "Go back and report to John what you have seen and heard: The blind receive sight, the lame walk, those who have leprosy are cured, the deaf hear, the dead are raised, and the good news is preached to the poor. Blessed is the man who does not fall away on account of me." (Luke 7:22,23)

PEACE—EVEN IN THE HOUR OF DEATH

"**D**id you hear what he said?" said one of John's followers to the others. "Why, he took credit for those healings. He claimed that he is the preacher of good tidings. And what's more, he maintained that it was he himself who raised those people from the dead. You know, I'm beginning to understand how our master, John, can face death so unafraid." Trusting in the Living Word, one need have no fear even when facing death.

Now we're down to brass tacks, down to the nitty gritty, aren't we? When we can maintain that believing the Word can bring power and peace, even when facing death, then we are talking about something both mighty and useful. It seems that everyone is afraid of death, or at least doesn't relish the thought of death too much. But the believer can banish all such fear and anxiety. He knows where he's going. He sees death for what it really is, that through the efforts of Jesus his Savior, death is the door to life eternal in heaven. The consolation which such knowledge brings is enough to give a man peace, even and especially, in the hour of death.

Look at John the Baptist. Imprisoned, certain death awaiting him, he nevertheless is calm. He sends his followers to hear from the Lord's own lips that it is he who is the long awaited Messiah. The Living Word has convinced him, and he knows that Christ's words will also be able to convince them. In the power of Christ's promise, John was ready to die in peace. Our Lord said of him, "Then what did you go out to see? A prophet? Yes, I tell you, and more than a prophet." When death came, John did not despair. He had Jesus' word. He could die in peace, for he believed his words.

That very same certainty that Christ has forgiven us our sins and that he will raise us from the dead will enable us to meet the hour of our own death without fear and trembling. Trusting in the one who will never fail us, we know that our departure here will be a glorious arrival there, where "He will wipe every tear from their eyes. There will be no more death or mourning or crying or pain, for the old order of things has passed away."

Let your Word comfort me in death and lead me to life. Amen.

84

When he had said this, Jesus called in a loud voice, "Lazarus, come out!" The dead man came out, his hands and feet wrapped with strips of linen, and a cloth around his face. Jesus said to them, "Take off the grave clothes and let him go." Therefore many of the Jews who had come to visit Mary, and had seen what Jesus did, put their faith in him. (John 11:43-45)

WHEN THE LORD CALLS US FROM THE GRAVE

"If Jesus had not called Lazarus by name," an elderly gentleman is quoted as saying, "the whole graveyard at Bethany would have emptied its tombs." Such is the power of a word from Jesus. He speaks, and the grip of death is broken. At the last day, say the Scriptures, "all who are in their graves will hear his voice, and come out."

Think of the scene at Bethany when, at the command of the Lord Jesus, Lazarus came walking out of a tomb that had held his dead, decaying body for four days. It's an astounding picture—Lazarus, the corpse, wrapped in grave clothes, stepping out of his tomb. Then transfer the picture to the day of judgment and imagine, if you can, the billions of graves in the world opening at one time and all the bodies coming out alive. From the small cemetery next to your church to the depths of the ocean, the dead will rise and will come before Jesus for the judgment, summoned by his voice.

There is at least one important difference between our rising on the last day and the raising of Lazarus. Lazarus was raised from the dead to continue this life until the natural processes of death took over again. We shall be raised in a glorified body that cannot die again. We see something of that difference indicated by the references to the grave clothes in the resurrections of Lazarus and of Jesus. Lazarus, still in his earthly body, came out of the tomb struggling with the clothes still wrapped around him. Jesus, in his glorified body, rose free from the grave clothes, which remained in place where his body had been lying. The glorified body will not be hindered by earthly things as our earthly bodies would be. We will have glorified bodies eternally free of decay and disease.

We will be like the Lord who will call us from the grave. We will "see him as he is." We will be caught up to meet him in the clouds of heaven and will live with him forever. Joy and thanksgiving will fill our hearts. For us and all who believe in Christ it will be a wonderful day when the Lord commands all the dead to come forth.

Come quickly, Lord Jesus. Amen.

Then Jesus told him, "Because you have seen me, you have believed; blessed are those who have not seen and yet have believed." (John 20:29)

FAITH WITHOUT SIGHT

Thomas believed because he saw. In our case, "Faith comes from hearing the message, and the message is heard through the word of Christ" (Romans 10:17). The bliss and happiness of saving faith does not rest upon the evidence of the senses, upon our feelings or even our reason, but alone on the word of the gospel. The Word of God brings Christ to us; the Word of God brings us to Christ.

Jesus approved the firm confession of Thomas with a word that shines like a beacon down through the centuries: "Because you have seen me, you have believed; blessed are those who have not seen and yet have believed." The words were spoken for our benefit. Jesus is not making a comparison between the faith of Thomas, who was privileged to see, and the faith of those who have not seen. As it is with us, Thomas was saved by faith in Christ as the promised Messiah, the Son of God. Yet, the words of our text bestow a special blessing on those who do not enjoy the same opportunity of the first disciples.

Our Savior undoubtedly granted them visible proof of his resurrection because he wished them to have an impressive demonstration of his successful redemptive work. His personal appearance would sustain their courage in this early era of the New Testament Church.

The resurrection is a reality. We believe this. We need not see Jesus visibly or personally. The disciples saw him and reported it to us in God's own inspired Word. Our faith is not some vague dream or wishful thinking. Our confidence rests on the powerful testimony of God the Holy Ghost. Behind these words stand all the power, the love, the wisdom and the truth of our Creator and Savior. Can we ask for better assurance or stronger evidence of the reality of our salvation!

Peter was a witness to this whole episode involving Thomas. His comforting words to us have a familiar echo: "Though you have not seen [Jesus], you love him; and even though you do not see him now, you believe in him and are filled with an inexpressible and glorious joy, for you are receiving the goal of your faith, the salvation of your souls" (1 Peter 1:8,9).

Gracious Savior, nourish our faith with your Word until we share in the fullness of your glory in heaven. Amen.

So the women hurried away from the tomb, afraid yet filled with joy, and ran to tell his disciples. (Matthew 28:8)

BRIGHT WITH JOY

A funeral director once commented, "I can tell when a grieving family comes into my establishment whether they are Christian or not. Christians have an altogether different way of handling their grief. There's a certain peace, almost an inner joy, even when they mourn."

The women who had met the angel at the tomb exemplify what that funeral director had observed. As they left the tomb, they were afraid. Perhaps their fear was the result of seeing a holy angel. Maybe the fear was that they would never be believed, or that what the angel had said was too good to be true. We are told that they felt that normal human emotion we call fear.

But that fear did not prevent them from being "filled with joy." Joy overcame their fears. Joy gave swiftness to their feet. It was the resurrection of Jesus that provided that fear-conquering joy. The grave was empty. Jesus had left it, using the power that he has over death. Gradually the meaning of the event must have occurred to them. Jesus lives! Death couldn't hold him. Then death has lost its hold on us, too!

The resurrection of Christ is the source of Christian joy. To be sure, Christians can and do often weep over the death of loved ones. But the tears shed by Christians over one who is now "asleep in Jesus" do not change the joy that is in their heart; in fact, it is that joy that comforts the Christian even as he mourns. It is joy over the fact of Christ's resurrection that keeps tears of sorrow from becoming tears of bitterness or despair, as must be the case with the nonbeliever.

The resurrection joy is a joy that fills the Christian's life. It doesn't come and go. In fact, it can't be shattered, even when tragedy strikes. It is a lasting joy, because it enables us to look past all the present sorrows and see our resurrected Lord, the Lord who promised, "Now is your time of grief, but I will see you again and you will rejoice, and no one will take away your joy."

Lord Jesus, your victory over death has filled us with joy. Lead us by the brightness of the resurrection to the eternal joy that you have prepared for us in heaven. Amen.

Jesus replied, "Go back and report to John what you hear and see: The blind receive sight, the lame walk, those who have leprosy are cured, the deaf hear, the dead are raised, and the good news is preached to the poor." (Matthew 11:4,5)

WHAT'S REALLY IMPORTANT

"**M**essiah!" "Son of God!" "Savior!" The works of Jesus shouted out: "Here is the one you were waiting for!" Were the individual miracles important? Ask the once blind Bartimaeus as he reads the *Jerusalem Times* over a cup of coffee! Ask the Samaritan leper hugging his wife after a hard day at the office. There hadn't been much hugging in the leper colony! Go to the parents, sisters, brothers and friends of the healed and the risen. Do you hear them singing? Can you see the lame man dancing? Each wonder touched tens and hundreds; each wonder was important in itself.

But, and we must hastily add this, the miracles were even more important as signs of who Jesus was. Jesus wanted, yes, he still wants, to be accepted not as a miracle-worker, but even more as the Savior from eternal death. Jesus used words to present himself to the world as the Savior, but he used works to prove that he was the Messiah the Old Testament predicted, and, therefore, our Savior.

To those who had trouble believing the words he would say, "At least believe me on account of the works."

The substance of Jesus, that is, the real, important stuff, was not and is not salvation from physical lameness, blindness or even death. The lame who walked, the blind who saw and the dead who rose remained sinners—sinners who would die and were headed for an unbearable eternity. No, the substance is the good news preached to poor and rich alike. It is news of a much more important salvation. It is the guarantee of a resurrection to eternal life, because the one who proclaimed the news also established it by turning away God's punishment from man back upon himself.

Let's keep our spiritual glasses on! To be healed is wonderful; to seek Jesus' help in physical distress is God's will for us. To be raised for a time is cause to jump and shout. But to live forever in God's presence is the true substance of the good news. And it is ours for the believing!

Lord Jesus, David's Son and Lord, keep our eyes turned heavenward. Deliver us from evils of body; but, most of all deliver us from hell's eternal evils. We praise your great salvation. Amen.

"The Counselor, the Holy Spirit, whom the Father will send in my name, will teach you all things and will remind you of everything I have said to you." (John 14:26)

LISTEN AS GOD SPEAKS

"Sure! You Christians quote from the Bible. But the Bible was written by men. And men can make mistakes."

That is what the unbeliever says. With that kind of reasoning the unbeliever tries to shake the Christian's faith and tries to make the Bible look like an unreliable book. But in today's Scripture verse Jesus himself contradicts that mistaken human opinion.

We all know how quickly people can forget what happened. We all know how quickly people can get the facts and the details mixed up. If the apostles had been left to themselves, they also would have misrepresented many of the things that Jesus said and did. If the disciples had been left on their own, they would have gotten the facts and the details mixed up. Their writings and their teachings would have been filled with all sorts of contradictions.

But God did not permit this to happen. Jesus did not let them wander off on their own. But it happened to them as he said in our Scripture lesson, "The Holy Spirit will remind you of everything I have said to you." The Holy Spirit caused the New Testament writers to remember exactly what Jesus had spoken and exactly what Jesus had done. The words which they spoke and wrote were given by inspiration of God the Holy Spirit. Therefore we have the assurance that the Bible is an accurate record of the Savior's words and deeds. It is the truth.

Therefore let us not idly sit back and hope that God will somehow appear to us or directly inform us of his will. If we want to hear God speak and be assured that it is truly God, and not the devil, speaking, we must go to his Word, the Bible. For that is where Jesus comes to us and makes himself known to us. We can hear and read the Bible with the confidence that Jesus himself is standing before us and instructing us. When the Bible reveals our sinfulness and our need for a Savior, Jesus is speaking. When the Bible tells us that "God so loved the world that he gave his only-begotten Son," Jesus himself is offering us his comfort. Let us then be eager to hear and to read the words of that sacred Book. And let us believe them.

Dear Savior, thank you for coming to us in your Word. Give us hearts that are eager to hear and to learn and to believe it. Amen.

Jesus answered, "I tell you the truth, no one can enter the kingdom of God unless he is born of water and the Spirit. Flesh gives birth to flesh, but the Spirit gives birth to spirit." (John 3:5,6)

BORN-AGAIN CHRISTIANS

What does it mean to be "born again"? Nicodemus had a problem understanding that, and there are people today who have a similar problem. There are those who claim to be "born-again Christians." We are happy to hear anyone confess allegiance to Christ, but we wonder a bit about the use of the term "born again." The implication seems to be that there are two kinds of Christians, those who are born again and those who are not. Some say that to be a real Christian one must be able to point to an extraordinary emotional experience at some specific time and place; without such a "Damascus road decision for Christ" a person is not a Christian in the full sense of the word.

But in its true scriptural sense to be born again simply means to become a believer in Christ. Everyone who has been brought to faith in the Savior is thus a born-again Christian. To this spiritual rebirth we contribute as little as we did to our natural birth into this world. The Holy Spirit, and he alone, is the Lord and Giver of life. He regenerates spiritually dead sinners who cannot by their own reason or strength believe in Jesus Christ, their Lord, or come to him. It is not our decision for Christ but the Spirit's gracious and powerful working in our hearts that gives us a new birth.

How does the Holy Spirit accomplish this miracle of regeneration? Through the means of grace, the gospel in word and sacraments. For most of us our spiritual rebirth took place when we were baptized as babies. There we were born again of water and Spirit, called into the kingdom of grace, made children of God and heirs of heaven. We need not look for some other unique or spectacular experience. All of the wonderful promises of the triune God apply to us whom the Spirit has called to faith by the gospel, God's power for our salvation.

May we appreciate the Spirit's work, and may we continue to use the Spirit's means so that our faith may be nourished and sustained. The Spirit does indeed work where and when he pleases, but always and only through the means of grace. That means is readily available to us. It is as close as our Bible, as close as the church pew, the baptismal font and the communion rail. God's grace is there for us to enjoy in the gospel. May we come and get it.

O Holy Spirit, enter in and in our hearts thy work begin. Amen.

"Go, tell his disciples and Peter, 'He is going ahead of you into Galilee. There you will see him, just as he told you.' " (Mark 16:7)

BENEFITING FROM GOD'S PROMISES

It is incredible how all the people who deny the physical resurrection of Jesus disregard the many undeniable proofs of it. From the testimony of eyewitnesses to the silence of his enemies, evidence abounds to support the fact that Jesus returned to life.

Just as incredible is the way that Jesus' followers were shocked and surprised by his resurrection. Jesus had told them, right from the start, that he was going to rise again. They had the promise of Easter. Mary Magdalene had the promise—and assumed Jesus' body was stolen. The disciples had the promise—and locked their doors in fear. Thomas had the promise—and demanded to see and touch.

The promise was there for them, but they did not benefit from it because they did not accept it by faith. Even when the empty tomb demonstrated that the promise had been fulfilled, they were slow to believe. That's a mistake that should be easy for us to avoid. We can start with Easter. We know that God has fulfilled that promise for us already. We rejoice that Jesus has risen.

But let's not stop there. God promises to hear and answer the prayers of his people, and he never fails to keep that promise. So we are encouraged to come before the throne of grace often with our petitions and thanksgivings.

God promises to forgive all our sins. He has told us the death of Christ was full payment for all sins. He guaranteed this in Jesus' resurrection. Cast your guilt at Jesus' feet and draw on the grace of God for daily comfort.

God promises to look after us in this world. His angels watch over us. He sustains us in every suffering and makes all things work together for our good. Rely on him and his love no matter how dark the road or painful the trial.

All these promises have been fulfilled for us. But one remains, the promise of heaven. Don't wait for Jesus to return before you believe. Put your faith in him now for your promised eternal salvation. Enjoy the blessings of knowing that paradise waits for us before the promise is changed to fulfillment. Then you will daily know and experience the great changes that the empty tomb of Jesus has brought about.

As we believe your promises, O Lord, give us comfort, peace, and joy that will be perfected when you take us to yourself in heaven. Amen.

The kingdom of heaven is like a landowner who went out early in the morning to hire men to work in his vineyard. . . . About the third hour he went out and saw others standing in the marketplace doing nothing. . . . He went out again about the sixth hour and the ninth hour and did the same thing. About the eleventh hour he went out and found still others standing around. (Matthew 20:1,3,5,6)

CALLED AT DIFFERENT TIMES

Some years ago I sat at the bedside of an elderly man in the hospital. He had asked me to pray for him. I was very glad and thankful for his request. I was also amazed. A few weeks ago when I came into this same room to visit a fellow Christian, this man shook his head and said, "I don't want any part of that religious nonsense!" My visits continued, and thankfully the condition of our Christian friend in the bed next to this aged man improved. Although he didn't want to admit it, this often crotchety man listened to our devotions.

It was on the day that our friend was moved to another room that this man asked me to pray for him. The power of the Word had had its desired effect. Over the next weeks I had the privilege of sharing the rich blessings of God's Word and the great treasure of forgiveness with a now willing listener. On one bright afternoon the man confided, "I'm glad the Lord didn't give up on me. I'm so happy he called me even at this late date." Jesus had indeed been patiently knocking at the door of his heart and finally entered by the Spirit's power.

God calls his people into the kingdom at different times. For some of us it is early in our lives at the time of our baptism. For others it is during the young searching years of life. For still others, it comes at a time when all others have given up on the person, all others except God, that is. Think of the Apostle Paul. God called him to preach the gospel to the Gentiles. This calling amazed a lot of people, for Paul had been a zealous persecutor of the Lord's church.

Remember that God has set us aside for himself before the world began. He who numbers our days knows those who are his. Even though human reason cannot see hope for someone, God knows that hope will live in the hearts of those he calls—no matter how late in life. Thank God for his persistent grace! Keep sharing the message of that grace—even with those who at first say, "No."

Merciful Lord, let us never underestimate the power of your grace upon our lives. Let us never tire of sharing the message of your love through Jesus, even when we wonder if if does any good. Amen.

Then they worshiped him and returned to Jerusalem with great joy. (Luke 24:52)

JOY!

Like a golden stream, the theme of joy runs from one end of the Bible to the other. "You [O Lord] will fill me with joy in your presence," says the Psalmist David. "With joy you will draw water from the wells of salvation," writes the Prophet Isaiah. "You will rejoice," says Jesus, "and no one will take away your joy." "I am full of joy," declares the Apostle Paul.

We are also told that immediately following Jesus' ascension into heaven, the disciples "returned to Jerusalem with great joy." It would seem that they had little reason for joy, especially not for "great joy." Their Savior had just vanished from their sight. They would never see him again this side of eternity. They also knew that ahead of them lay persecution and even death. Jesus had told them to expect this. They knew that many would reject their message. On top of all that, they were returning to Jerusalem, the hotbed of opposition to Jesus and everything he stood for.

Yet they returned "with great joy." Why? There were many reasons. Although they no longer saw Jesus, they knew he was still with them. His returning to heaven was another instance of his keeping his word; he had said he would go there to prepare a place for them. And, in spite of all the problems they would face, Jesus had promised them their work would be successful. He had given them the astounding promise, "I tell you the truth, anyone who has faith in me will do what I have been doing. He will do even greater things than these, because I am going to the Father. And I will do whatever you ask in my name."

In this life we can be sure we will have our share of troubles. At the same time we can rejoice with the disciples—and for the same reasons. Jesus is with us, though we don't see him. He is preparing a place for us, and will bring us to himself someday. God's Word assures us that our work for him is never in vain.

The psalmist aptly described the joy of Christ's ascension, when he wrote long before the event: "God has ascended amid shouts of joy!" Long after the event we have every reason to live joyful lives. Our Savior, who has won our salvation, is now ruling over all things and using them for our eternal good. Let us do all within our power to share that joy with others!

Jesus, our ascended Lord, amid life's troubles keep us from losing sight of the lasting joy we have in you. Amen.

While he was blessing them, he left them and was taken up into heaven. (Luke 24:51)

"HE LEFT THEM"

"**H**e left them." These three little words sum up one of the most momentous moments in the history of our planet.

For thirty-three years Immanuel—"God with us"—had lived among us. Clothed in human flesh, the almighty, eternal God became our brother. The Apostle John describes how he and the other disciples "have heard, . . . have seen with our eyes . . . and our hands have touched" God incarnate, God in-the-flesh. Not only did he take on our flesh and blood, but Jesus Christ also took on our sorrows and our griefs. He became like us in all things, except that he was without sin. He, the innocent one, laid down his life for us the sinners.

Now we read that "he left them." Now the bringer of joy and life no longer walks among us. No longer can the sick feel the physical touch of his healing hand. No longer can his disciples hear his reassuring voice or see the forgiving look of love in his eyes.

"He left them." But notice that Luke does not say, "He deserted them." Far from it. It was not Christ's purpose merely to tease the world with a brief moment of heavenly light and love. He is visibly gone but has not left us alone. He has promised to send us the Holy Spirit, the Comforter. And Jesus has also promised his own unseen presence with the words, "Surely I am with you always."

"He left them." Some people have a sense of confidence from the fact that they do not see God. They think it means that God doesn't see them either, and so they can ignore God's commandments. This is wicked and foolish thinking. For even though Jesus has left the earth, he still sees everything that goes on here, including the very thoughts and desires of our hearts. Someday he will return to judge the world.

In the book of Acts Luke records how angels told the disciples, "This same Jesus, who has been taken from you into heaven, will come back in the same way you have seen him go."

"He left them." There's one more important truth here. When he left this world, Jesus did not leave his humanity behind. The almighty God is still our brother. He is preparing a place for us in heaven, that someday we may be with him. And he will never leave us.

O Savior, precious Savior, whom yet unseen we love, comfort us with the assurance that you are with us always. Hasten the day of your return, so that we may see you face to face. Amen.

And they stayed continually at the temple praising God. (Luke 24:53)

PRAISE GOD!

In the second chapter of his Gospel, St. Luke writes that when Jesus was born "a great company of the heavenly host appeared with the angel, praising God and saying, 'Glory to God in the highest. . . .' "

Today's Scripture passage is the closing verse of Luke's Gospel. A lot had happened in the thirty-three years since the angels praised God at the Savior's birth. Jesus had lived out his life on earth. He had completed his mission. He had suffered, died, risen again and ascended into heaven. And now, Luke tells us, it is the disciples of Jesus who are praising God. The angels knew the wonderful work that Jesus came to do; now the disciples knew it as an accomplished fact.

It is interesting that we find them praising God "at the temple." Jesus had told them to wait in Jerusalem until the Holy Spirit came to them. After he came, they were to go everywhere proclaiming the gospel. But for now they continually remained in the temple. This was where Jesus had taught when in Jerusalem, where he had chased out the merchants and the money-changers. Here he had been confronted by his enemies the Sadducees and Pharisees.

It must have felt strange for the disciples to return to the temple. As they watched the many sacrificial animals being offered there, they had to think of the supreme sacrifice for sin: Jesus' death on the cross. As they heard the Old Testament scriptures read, they could not but think of the fulfiller of all the prophecies. He had come and gone. As they thought about these things, the disciples could not but praise God.

According to one dictionary, to praise means "to commend the worth of." We can never say enough about the worth of Jesus and what he has done for us. He has done what all the world's gold and silver could not do—redeemed us from sin. He has done what all the world's wisdom and power cannot do—won for us eternal life.

May we follow the disciples' example. Let us live our lives for our ascended Lord and continually praise his name. At the right hand of God—that is, with almighty power—he rules over all creation. "Praise him for his acts of power," exalts the psalmist, "praise him for his surpassing greatness." Yes, yes, praise the Lord!

Oh, grant, dear Lord, this grace to me,
Recalling Thine ascension,
That I may ever walk with Thee,
Adorning Thy redemption.
And then, when all my days shall cease,
Let me depart in joy and peace,
In answer to my pleading. Amen.

At that time the king dom of heaven will be like ten virgins who took their lamps and went ou to meet the bridegroom. (Matthew 25:1)

EXPECTANT CHRISTIANS

Ten bridesmaids are waiting for a wedding reception to begin. Can you imagine a more carefree, excited group of people? The heavy responsibilities of preparing for the wedding went to someone else. All they had to do was stand there and look pretty. Now the serious part of the ceremony is over and the fun part is about to begin: to laugh and play and eat and drink, perhaps till the wee hours of the morning. These bridesmaids have everything to look forward to, whether the wedding takes place at the time of Christ, or in the twentieth century.

Jesus compares these excited bridesmaids to his disciples, the members of the holy Christian church on earth. They are looking forward to something far better than a wedding reception. They are looking forward to the glories of heaven.

Jesus has promised that he will return. "I am going there to prepare a place for you. And if I go and prepare a place for you, I will come back and take you to be with me that you also may be where I am." The Revelation of St. John describes heaven as a beautiful city with streets of gold so pure that it shines like glass, filled with light that proceeds from God himself, where saints and angels sing joyful praises to the Lamb who poured out his blood for their salvation.

That's what Christians are looking forward to. That's what you and I are looking forward to. And when we think about it like that, the prospect of our Lord's return is far more exciting than a wedding reception. For this is one celebration that's going to last forever!

At the same time Christians are not only looking forward. They're also looking backward, at the grief and misery that surrounds them in this world. Not only the unemployment and poverty and disease and death, but also man's inhumanity to man, the baby-killing, the child abuse, the broken marriages and broken minds and spirits that come from broken homes. And on top of all this an immorality that scorns the Christian sense of right and wrong, a value system that makes mockery of the treasures of salvation that God has given us. And the sorrow of seeing fellow Christians swept away by the mounting ungodliness, until we say, "If God does not shorten these days how shall even God's elect be saved?"

The bridesmaids waiting to get into the wedding reception are not nearly as eager to get in as Christians who are waiting for the return of their heavenly Bridegroom.

Come quickly, Lord Jesus, come quickly. Amen.

**"Do not let your hearts be troubled. Trust in God; trust also in me."
(John 14:1)**

FACING THE FUTURE WITH FAITH

It was going to be a night of doubt and despair for the Twelve. It was the night of Jesus' betrayal and trial and sentence of death. Before twenty-four hours had passed he would be crucified, dead and buried. They would wonder if they could still think of him as Savior, whether God was still their loving Father. They had been so secure in his company while he taught the multitudes and healed the sick and raised the dead. But before morning they would see him arrested and degraded.

To prepare them for that terrible experience which would tempt them to despair, Jesus said: "Trust in God; trust also in me." My Father can be trusted. He has always proved himself to be trustworthy. I can be trusted. Place your confidence in me and don't let panic rob your hearts of faith.

There are things in our future which we cannot foresee. But we know from the Word of God and from human experience that our lives can change so quickly. Today prosperous and secure, tomorrow unemployed. Today cheerful and content, tomorrow broken and weak. Today confident in the loving concern of our Savior, tomorrow wondering whether he still cares.

It is just that last condition that he wants to prevent by speaking these words of our text to his disciples and leaving them for us in the pages of Holy Scripture. "Do not let your hearts be troubled."

Don't leap to any false conclusions about me and my concern for you. I cared enough to join the human race when I could have just continued in my majesty forever. I suffered for the human race, suffered more than you will ever suffer. I did my Father's will and finished my Father's work. I carried out his plan for your salvation as your Representative before his bar of justice. He raised me again to demonstrate that his justice is satisfied and you are forgiven. See my hands and my side, my empty tomb. Can you doubt my good will?

"You trust in God; trust also in me." The important thing to concentrate on here is that he is strong and loving. We quickly find out how weak our faith is. But our God is strong. It is not that we are so good at trusting, but that he is trustworthy. Where shall we find confidence for the future? In his cross, his empty grave.

**Who shall help us in the strife
Lest the Foe confound us?
Thou only, Lord, Thou only. Amen.**

"In my Father's house are many rooms; if it were not so, I would have told you. I am going there to prepare a place for you." (John 14:2)

THERE IS A PLACE FOR YOU!

Have you ever felt "out of place"—perhaps at a party, in a new school or in a strange neighborhood? The feeling that you just don't belong is not a pleasant one, is it? But you don't feel "out of place" in your own home, do you? You know you belong there. And you don't feel out of place at your church, do you? You know you belong there, too. And today Jesus assures us that in heaven we will also feel right at home, for heaven is our Father's house, and there is a nice, cozy place for each of us there.

Heaven is our Father's house. Our loving Creator dwells there. Our loving Savior is also there. And the Spirit who sanctifies us is there. The holy angels who watch over us are there, and all of our loved ones who have fallen asleep in Christ are there.

Heaven is a large house. It has many rooms, Jesus says. He does not say exactly how many rooms our heavenly mansion has, but it must be very many. In the Revelation to St. John Jesus reveals that heaven is like a vast, holy city. He describes its dimensions as over 1,400 miles wide, by 1,400 miles long, by 1,400 miles high. That would mean that one side of this heavenly cube is equal to half the distance from New York to Los Angeles. If we estimate that each story of the city is fifteen feet high, the city would have 528 stories. Thus, the total square footage of heaven would be 1,188,000,000,000 square miles. If we would divide that by the total estimated population of the world since the beginning of time (about 30,000,000,000), that would leave 198 square miles for every family! Now, of course, this picture of the heavenly city is a symbolic picture not to be taken literally, but it does symbolize a heaven with plenty of room for everyone.

You may still think that you will feel out of place in heaven since it is a holy place occupied by the holy God, holy angels and holy saints. And you know very well that you are totally sinful. Won't you be out of place there? Not at all! Jesus went to Calvary to prepare a place in heaven for you. He paid for all your sin. Don't be afraid of moving in to your new heavenly home! God has declared you holy because of Jesus' perfect life, death and resurrection. Heaven is your home. There is a place for you there.

Precious Savior, thank you for preparing a room in heaven for me. Amen.

"Do not let your hearts be troubled. Trust in God ; trust also in me. In my Father's house are many rooms; if it were not so, I would have told you. I am going there to prepare a place for you. And if I go and prepare a place for you, I will come back and take you to be with me that you also may be where I am. (John 14:1-3)

CHRIST WILL COME AGAIN TO TAKE US HOME

The parable of the ten virgins points out that there was only distress and everlasting misery in store for the five who foolishly failed to have oil in their lamps. The bridegroom's sudden arrival caught them unprepared. Any last moment attempt to correct the past came too late. The door was shut. That was final. "Then they will go away to eternal punishment" (Matthew 25:46).

"The door was shut." That is a hard sentence. Does it apply to us? How dreadful if that were the case! The selfsame Bridegroom who shut the door to the foolish also said, "Come, you who are blessed by my Father; take your inheritance, the kingdom prepared for you since the creation of the world" (Matthew 25:34).

When we view our life in the light of God's holy commandments, we have reason to stand in dread of "the Great Day of the Lord." We have sinned and come short of the glory of God (Romans 3:27). We would despair if God's Word did not tell us, "Blessed is he whose transgressions are forgiven, whose sins are covered" (Psalm 32:1).

This is our comfort and joy. The Bridegroom, our Savior Jesus Christ, has completely covered our sins. Clothed in the garment of his righteousness we have nothing to fear. His promise goes far beyond our fondest hopes and dreams. Not only are we assured that God no longer sees our guilt, but our Savior also promises us a place in heaven with him! More than that. He tells us that he himself has prepared this place for us. And when our last hour shall come, when we walk through the valley of the shadow of death, we know that he will be at our side. His promise is: "I go and prepare a place for you; I will come back and take you to be with me that you also may be where I am." There is no greater promise than that!

Whatever tribulations the Christian may have to endure as a faithful witness of Christ here on earth, the promise of God removes all weeping and sighing, for "the Lamb at the center of the throne will be their shepherd; he will lead them to springs of living water. And God will wipe away every tear from their eyes" (Revelation 7:17).

Be Thou at my right hand,
Then can I never fail.
Uphold Thou me, and I shall stand;
Fight Thou, and I'll prevail. Amen.

Do not let your hearts be troubled. Trust in God; trust also in me. (John 14:1)

TRUST ME!

"Just trust me! I know what I'm doing!" Tom's wife was afraid that his decision to change careers would only result in financial hardship and more unhappiness for the family. But Tom insisted that he knew what he was doing. If his family would just trust him!

We have often heard the same words from a family member when making a financial investment, choosing a travel route or making an important decision. Experience has shown that people may not always know what they are doing, but there is one who can always be trusted.

"Just trust me," is what Jesus said to his disciples in the Upper Room on the night before his crucifixion. Their hearts were deeply troubled that night. They were confused by Jesus' solemn announcement that he would suffer, die and rise again. They were frightened and disturbed by Jesus' declaration that he would soon go away and leave them. They were shaken by Jesus' disclosure that one of them would betray him. The future looked bleak. On what strange course was the Lord leading them? Was he doing the right thing? Would it only end in disaster for him—and them?

We can understand how they felt that night. There have been, there may be now, or someday there will be moments when we wonder: "Is he leading me in the right direction? Does he know what he is doing?" In those moments our Savior still speaks to our troubled hearts: "Just trust me!"

In contrast to the troubled disciples, Jesus was remarkably calm that evening. He was fully aware of the anguish and agony which would soon come upon him as he sacrificed his holy life in payment for all sin, but he was not thinking of himself. Loving them to the end, he told his anxious and worried disciples: "Continue trusting in God . . . and continue to trust in me." Even in the shadows of suffering and death there was no need to fear. He knew what he was doing. He was still in control. "Just trust," he said, "everything will turn out well."

This is still true. He is always in control. Our Lord knows what he is doing. Don't be afraid—just trust him!

I am trusting Thee, Lord Jesus;
Never let me fall.
I am trusting Thee forever
And for all. Amen.